M000204721

"You will read and read . . . and read, through tears and laughter, while wondering how any man could be so astute, so tender, so frank, and so inspiring in speaking to his Christian sisters—whatever their position in life—of the glorious, fearful, humbling and immensely influential calling of the Christian woman. In these pages, written long ago, you will nonetheless find your mother, your sisters, your friends, and mostly yourself, as you hear the passionate voice of a godly pastor and tender brother calling you to repent, to take heart, to reconsider, to resist, and to persevere in the life of humility and love to which you are called in Christ."

—REBECCA CLOWNEY JONES
*Wife and Mother*
*Author, "Does Christianity Squash Women?"*

Without a doubt Adolphe Monod is my favorite French author of the nineteenth century: in his writings one sees such devotion to God and such desire to bring glory to his Savior, the Lord Jesus! This volume, which touches on a subject of perennial interest, is no exception. What is especially striking about this study of God's intent in the creation of woman is Monod's determination to follow the Scriptures in all that they say about women and their role in the family and the larger world. Not surprisingly there is material in this volume that runs counter to the wisdom of our culture: so be it! May this new translation of this old classic study be the means of helping us hear afresh God's Word for our day.

—MICHAEL HAYKIN
*Southern Baptist Theological Seminary*

Adolphe Monod was one of the brightest lights in the French Awakening of the 19th century. On the surface this text shows him to be a child of his times. But underneath, it is a passionate defense of the biblical view which sees men and women as ontologically equal and yet economically different. That is, in their being as God's creatures they are equally image-bearers. In their functions and responsibilities they are complementary. In Constance Walker's translation the text is as alive in English as it is in the original French. This text is required reading for the present conversation.

—WILLIAM EDGAR
*Westminster Theological Seminary, Philadelphia*

In this treasure of a book, Monod makes crystal clear that the godly woman's overarching mission is to glorify God. Under that ultimate mission, Monod clarifies how the godly woman is to do that specifically. He calls it her "distinctive mission." He says, "Do not count on the world to clarify this mission for you. It has never known it and cannot understand it." He calls on the reader to "rely on God's Word." Skillfully unpacking the Word of God, Monod strikingly and specifically communicates the "distinctive mission" of the Godly woman. . . . This book will equip you for your ultimate mission to glorify God and clarify your distinctive mission as a faithful woman.

—LORI RHODES
*Wife and Mother*
*Nourishment for Ladies (www.nitw4ladies.blogspot.com)*

Monod's work, although written well over 100 years ago, remains applicable today because it is based on biblical truth. It is so important, but so challenging, for me to let God's Word guide how I interpret my culture, rather than letting my culture guide how I interpret God's Word. As a single woman and a young attorney, Monod's book encouraged me to seek my identity beneath the cross of Christ and to find my worth in His love for me, rather than in my circumstances. Although sometimes driven by his culture and time, the vast majority of Monod's interpretation of the biblical role of a woman rang true to my innate desires and my own reading of the Bible. I would encourage readers to consider it humbly and prayerfully, looking for how God might direct them in application. One of my favorite quotes was, "To be loved is the joy of your heart . . . but to love, to devote yourself through love, is the need of your soul" (p 32).

—SARAH
*Young attorney (J.D., M.S.W.)*

# Woman

## HER MISSION
## AND HER LIFE

## OTHER TITLES BY ADOLPHE MONOD

*Living in the Hope of Glory*
"Monod's dying testimony is instructing, enriching, inspiring."
—RICK PHILLIPS

*An Undivided Love*
"With unequaled passion and clarity he brings the unassuming listener not merely to the foot of the cross, but to Jesus himself."
—WILLIAM EDGAR

*Jesus Tempted in the Wilderness*
"Adolphe Monod at his best. It is a masterpiece.
You really must read this book."
—JOEL R. BEEKE

## FORTHCOMING TITLE

*Saint Paul*
(Five Discourses on Paul's impact and example, designed to help reignite the Church to transform today's world.)

# *Woman*

## HER MISSION
## AND HER LIFE

NEW SECTION:
FOUR MONOD WOMEN

# ADOLPHE MONOD

CONSTANCE K. WALKER
EDITOR AND TRANSLATOR

SOLID GROUND
CHRISTIAN BOOKs
P.O. BOX 660132 • VESTAVIA HILLS • ALABAMA 35266

© 2011 by Constance K. Walker

All rights reserved. No part of this book may be reproduced, stored in a retrieval system, or transmitted in any form or by any means—electronic mechanical, photocopy, recording, or otherwise—except for brief quotations for the purpose of review or comment, without the prior permission of the publisher, Solid Ground Christian Books, P.O. Box 660132, Vestavia Hills, Alabama 35266.

Unless otherwise indicated, all Scripture quotations are taken from The Holy Bible, English Standard Version (denoted as ESV), copyright © 2001 by Crossway Bibles, a division of Good News Publishers. Used by permission. All rights reserved.

Scripture quotations marked KJV are taken from the Authorized (King James) Version of the Holy Bible.

*Cover image courtesy of Ken Jenkins*
*[For other examples of his work, please visit www.kenjenkins.com.]*

*Cover design by Borgo Design*

Printed in the United States of America

978-159925-260-5

TRANSLATOR'S DEDICATION

*For my sisters in the Lord*

# CONTENTS

Adolphe Monod, 1802–1856

# Biographical Sketch

Adolphe Monod (1802–1856) has rightly been called "The Voice of the Awakening." Those who came out of curiosity to hear the preaching of a celebrated orator would often leave the service pierced to the heart by his message, while the mature Christians in his congregations came back again and again to be transported by his preaching into the very presence of God and to have their faith stretched and challenged. Others, including Adolphe's older brother, Frédéric, were more influential as leaders of the movement that swept across France and Switzerland in the early 19th century, but none could expound the central core of its faith quite as clearly or persuasively or appealingly as Adolphe Monod.

Yet Monod's faith did not come without a struggle. He was descended from protestant ministers and received a clear call to the ministry at age fourteen, but the faith he grew up with was more formal than vibrant. In 1820 he entered seminary in Geneva, where the varied theological viewpoints soon left him in a state of spiritual confusion. He was often drawn toward the teaching of the Awakening, especially as presented by a Scotsman named Thomas Erskine, but his reason could not accept all of its teachings. Still confused, he accepted ordination in 1824.

Confusion turned to crisis when he agreed to pastor a group of French-speaking Protestants in Naples. He knew he could not express his doubts to the congregation, but his natural candor recoiled at preaching something he did not yet believe. Family members prayed earnestly for him, and once again he received help through a visit by Thomas Erskine.

Eventually, on July 21, 1827, he reached a state of peace. "I wanted to make my own religion, instead of taking it from God. . . . I was without God and burdened with my own well being, while now I have a God who carries the burden for me. That is enough." He still had questions, but he knew he would find the answers in the pages of the Bible.

Shortly thereafter he was called to join the pastoral staff of the large but worldly Reformed Church in Lyon, where his bold, gospel-centered preaching soon drew opposition. He was told not to preach salvation by grace; he refused. They demanded his resignation; he refused. After much unpleasantness, the leaders secured the government's permission to dismiss him, but a group of evangelical Christians who had already left the national church asked him to establish an independent congregation in Lyon. He served there until an unexpected call led him to the national church's seminary in Montauban. A decade later, in 1847, he returned to the pastorate, serving the Reformed Church in Paris. Quite ill and diagnosed with terminal cancer in 1855, he began holding small communion services in his home. These continued until his death on April 6, 1856, with his children writing down and then publishing the brief meditations he gave.

Those facts, however, fail to truly capture the spirit of the man. His was a strong and passionate faith, in part because of his early spiritual struggles. He was also a man of great integrity, a keen mind, and a deeply caring, pastoral heart. All of these qualities were augmented and set off by his natural gift for speaking. Yet even as his renown grew, Adolphe Monod remained a truly humble man. A week before his death he said, "I have a Savior! He has freely saved me through his shed blood, and I want it to be known that I lean uniquely on that poured out blood. All my righteous acts, all my works which have been praised, all my preaching that has been appreciated and sought after—all that is in my eyes only filthy rags."

# TRANSLATOR'S PREFACE

Society today is telling women that we can "have it all." Marriage, career, children, hobbies—we can cram it all in and *should* cram it all in if we want to live fulfilled lives. We are encouraged to build our careers around male models, which reward long hours and high pressure situations, while short-changing personal and family time. But are we really more fulfilled? Or are we simply more exhausted, more burned out?

More importantly, what is the Bible telling us? What kind of nature did God put into us? And for what purpose? Over 150 years ago, Adolphe Monod addressed these questions in a pair of sermons printed here in a new translation. This is a peaceful, thoughtful book that I hope will resonate with its readers, especially its female readers. Parts of it may sound almost revolutionary (or maybe antiquated!) to our 21$^{st}$ century ears, and some of the applications will not be directly relevant, yet it is worth pondering these fundamental issues from a biblical perspective untainted by the spirit of our age.

When I accepted Christ in 1975 as a young physics professor, God immediately changed my priorities. My career fell well down on the list, even as God himself came to occupy first place. The process of learning to live out those new priorities in a way that honored God and allowed me better to serve my husband took much longer. I wish this book had been available to me then.

In 2003, Solid Ground Christian Books reprinted an 1852 translation of this monograph. Now, as part of a series of Monod's works, a new translation is being offered. The goal has been to produce an edition that is both more readable and more accurate than the earlier one.[1] Monod's footnotes are followed with his initials given in brackets [A.M.]; other footnotes have been supplied by the translator.

A new feature of this edition is a section showing how Adolphe Monod's teaching was exemplified in the lives of his wife Hannah, his mother Louise, his sister Adèle, and his daughter Sarah. This section is made up mainly of quotations from family correspondence and diaries.

The wildflowers in Ken Jenkins' cover image, "Bee Balm on a Summer Ridge," echo the single red flower adorning the previous edition of *Woman*, while here they assume the feminine role of humble servants. They attract our gaze, not to hold it, but to lead it away from them and out into the broader peaceful landscape.

I am once again indebted to my dear friend and writer of Christian fantasy, Sarah G. Byrd, for her critical review of the text and many helpful comments. I am also grateful to her daughter Sarah A. Byrd, who provided useful feedback and the viewpoint of a young professional woman, and to friend Gwillim Law, whose grammatical expertise and attention to detail were invaluable in the final editing.

It is my prayer that this new edition of *Woman* will bring peace and wholeness to my sisters in Christ who may be pondering, as I did years ago, how to live their lives in accordance with God's perfect design for them as women. May it also help its male readers to understand and appreciate the women in their lives, so that they can encourage them to fulfill their God-given mission.

Constance K. Walker
Durham, North Carolina

---

[1] The French text is from *Sermons par Adolphe Monod, Deuxième Édition, Troisième Série, Paris I* (Librairie de Ch. Meyrueis et Comp., Paris, 1859). This edition includes a small amount of editing that Monod did after the printing of the monograph that was the source for the 1852 translation.

*first discourse*

# HER MISSION

# HER MISSION

Genesis 2:18

Then the LORD God said, "It is not good that the man should be alone; I will make him a helper fit for him."

## WOMAN'S INFLUENCE

My dear sisters,

If it is you whom I address today, the rest of the audience, accustomed to seeing its name figure at the head of our discourses, has no cause for jealously. In speaking *to* woman and working to sanctify her influence, I am speaking *for* man.

Yes, her influence. In denying woman authority, which goes from the strong to the weak and is submitted to out of necessity, the Creator has accorded her influence, which typically goes from the weak to the strong and is freely accepted, but only on the condition that it is not at all evident.[1] I say

---

[1] This remark applies not only to different levels of the social or domestic hierarchy, but even to levels of ability. It is not, in general, the ordinary

without hesitation that the greatest influence existing on earth, for good or ill, is hidden in woman's hand.

## HER INFLUENCE IN HISTORY

History joins me in declaring woman's influence, even if the historian sometimes does not, either because he misconstrues this hidden undercurrent or because he keeps silent out of consideration for the self-love of one sex or the other.

Let us study past centuries. Nothing distinguishes the savage state from civilization, the East from the West, paganism from Christianity, antiquity from the Middle Ages, or the Middle Ages from modern times more truly than the condition of woman. For example, who does not know how much the single word polygamy or monogamy weighs on the morals and destiny of a people? If we observe what is going on around us, we will find woman everywhere in the world just as the poet depicts Agrippina in the senate, "behind a veil, invisible, yet present."[2]

As it was through a woman that Satan penetrated our innocent race, so one will commonly see traced to woman the calamities and crimes that desolate humanity—the hatred, vengeance, lawsuits, suicides, duels, murders, wars. And as it was through a woman that the Savior entered our fallen race, so one will equally see traced to woman the thoughts and deeds that lift up and console humanity—the tender devotions, generous sacrifices, holy inspirations, godly institutions, charitable foundations. Isn't that why art and poetry of all periods personify the moral powers as women and why in

---

spirit who submits to the influence of the eminent spirit; it is the reverse. This may seem like a paradox, but one will find, I believe, that when tested, it has experience on its side. [A.M.]

[2] From the opening scene of the play Britannicus by Jean Racine, first produced in 1669.

Proverbs the Holy Spirit himself depicts the two opposing tendencies that divide the world through the traits of two women?[3] Therefore imparting a healthy direction to woman's terrible influence by studying with her the mission she has received from God will serve the greatest interests of humanity.

## HER DISTINCTIVE MISSION

By your mission, my woman listeners, I mean here the distinctive mission of your sex. There is a general mission that you share with us. It is to represent on earth and thereby glorify the God who made us all in his image and who, on seeing that image effaced by sin, has renewed it in his Son. From this standpoint, just as "there is neither Jew nor Greek . . . neither slave nor free," so there is also "neither male nor female, for [we] are all one in Christ Jesus" (Galatians 3:28). But within that common mission, which must be the primary object of your ambition as well as ours, there is for you a special mission, one adapted to the way you were created.

Do not count on the world to clarify this mission for you. It has never known it and cannot understand it, because it has always reduced the question that concerns you to the petty proportions of its own egotism or your vanity. It remains for us to rely on God's Word, on that Word which, though fully preoccupied with setting forth "the one thing . . . necessary" (Luke 10:42), still resolves in passing all of humanity's great questions. Joining example with precept, it judges all things rightly because it judges them spiritually.[4]

---

[3] Chapter 7 (the adulteress) vs. chapter 8 (wisdom) and 9:1–12 (wisdom) vs. 9:13–18 (the woman Folly). [A.M.]

[4] "The natural person does not accept the things of the Spirit of God, for they are folly to him, and he is not able to understand them because they are spiritually discerned" (1 Corinthians 2:14). [A.M.]

I open the Word to the first pages of the first book, which is so aptly named Genesis, because it reveals the secret of all that exists[5] by intercepting it at its very origin. It playfully tosses the highest philosophy out to us in primitive facts set forth with a primitive naïveté. There, right after the little phrase where God summarizes the general mission of humanity—"Let us make man in our image" (Genesis 1:26)—we discover another little phrase where, before going on to form woman, he equally summarizes her special mission—"It is not good that the man should be alone; I will make him a helper fit for him" (Genesis 2:18). This applies to every woman, not just to the married woman, for Eve is not only the wife of the first man, she is also the first woman. Bound together with all of her sex, just as Adam is with ours, she offers in her person the prototype and a sort of miniature of all women.

Starting from this thought that presided at your birth, let us take as our guide in developing it the inspired instruments of both the old and new orders.[6] There is no risk of going astray on a path where God himself walks ahead of us. Moreover, in hearing what God's Word requires of you, your heart will complete the exposition and will compel you to say, "Yes, that really is what I ought to be; that really is what I ought to do."

## THE ORDER OF CREATION

### THE NEED FOR A HELPER

"It is not good that man should be alone." Filled up with God's gifts, he yet lacks something of which he himself is

---

[5] Literally "all existences."
[6] Literally "economies."

unaware or which he knows only through a vague intuition: "a helper fit for him." Without it, earth is for him but a place of solitude and Eden but a desert. Gifted with a nature that is too communicative to be self-sufficient, he cries out for a companion, a support, a complement, and he is only half alive as long as he lives alone. Made to think, to speak, to love, his thought seeks another thought to sharpen it and to reveal it to itself; his word is sadly lost in the air or awakens only an echo that mutilates it instead of responding to it; his love does not know what to do with itself and, falling back on itself, threatens to turn into distressing egotism. In the end, his entire being longs for another self.

But that other self does not exist. "There was not found a helper fit for him" (Genesis 2:20). The visible creatures around him are too far beneath him and the invisible being who gave him life is too far above him for them to unite their condition with his. Then God forms woman, and the great problem is resolved. There it is, just as Adam asked for it, that other self that is him and yet not him. Woman is a companion whom God has given to man to charm his existence and redouble it by sharing it. Her calling by birth is a calling of charity.

The place that God assigns for woman is related to this calling. It is not an inferior place. Woman is not simply a helper for man, she is a helper "fit for him."[7] She is to walk as his equal, and it is only in this way that she can bring him the help he needs. Yet she is given a secondary and dependant place, for woman was formed after man, made for man, and finally drawn forth from man. This last trait says it all to him. Drawn forth from him, she is "bone of his bones and flesh of his flesh" (see Genesis 2:23), and she is so closely united with him that he cannot disparage her without disparaging himself. Yet at the same time, drawn forth from

---

[7] The French version cited is literally "similar to him," or "like him."

him, she owes him the life that she breathes and the name that she bears. By what right—I should say, by what heart—would she dispute the highest rank with him? Her position by birth is a position of humility.

A calling of charity with regard to man in a position of humility beside man: that is woman's mission. Moreover, this calling and position, declared by the same facts and stemming from the same principle, are so inseparable in the formation of woman that they can be summed up in the single idea of renouncement, applied in turn to self-will and self-glory.

## SAINT PAUL'S COMMENTARY

I learned this commentary on Moses from Saint Paul as he recalls woman's condition to the Corinthians in order to justify forbidding her to pray or to prophesy with her head uncovered (1 Corinthians 11:1–13). His subject does not require him to expound on woman's calling of charity, so he limits himself to merely indicating it by noting that woman was created for man (1 Corinthians 11:9). But listen to the terms in which he explains himself on her position of humility. "I would have you know, that the head of every man is Christ; and the head of the woman is the man; and the head of Christ is God" (1 Corinthians 11:3 KJV).[8] "Man . . . is the image and glory of God, but woman is the glory of man. For man was not made from woman, but woman from man" (1 Corinthians 11:7–8).

Is this not the doctrine I just found in Genesis? But the apostle expresses it with a strictness that would be out of

---

[8] The King James Version quoted here follows the French version of the Bible quoted by Adolphe Monod and most of the older translations of the Bible. The English Standard Version has ". . . the head of a wife is her husband. . . ." The Greek language uses the same word for both woman and wife, as is the common practice in French.

place in any other mouth, and for the general idea of dependence at which I stopped, he substitutes the more precise notion of subordination.[9] From this, he concludes that, "because of the angels" (1 Corinthians 11:10) who watch what is happening on earth and especially in the church (Ephesians 3:10), woman "ought to have a symbol of [the] authority" under which she is placed "on her head" (1 Corinthians 11:10). Man, whose birth is part of the great work of creation that inspires shouts of joy among the angels (Job 38:7), being the image and glory of God, owes it to God to show himself in the eyes of the whole universe with his head lifted up. On the other hand, woman, whose formation is a secondary event and, so to speak, a family matter, being the glory of man, owes it to man to hold herself hidden in the relatively narrow surroundings of our globe, like a modest wife inside her home (Genesis 18:9).

The apostle's intent is that much clearer because the instructions he gives here are destined for exceptional women, for it is only by an exception that a woman could be called to pray or prophesy before men. The order that God has established toward a certain end, he is always free to modify in order to better serve that end. Sometimes, in the interests of man, we see him pushing a woman out of the path he has prescribed for women. It may be to prophesy like the women of Corinth, the four daughters of the deacon Philip (Acts 21:9), or the mother of King Lemuel (Proverbs 31:1); or it may be to judge the people as Deborah did (Judges 4:4–5), or even to preside over a military campaign (Judges 4 and 5). Then the woman can only obey, and she will be blessed in her obedience. "Most blessed of women be Jael, the wife of Heber the Kenite, of tent-dwelling women most blessed" (Judges 5:24). But even then, apart from what

---

[9] In the next section, Adolphe Monod shows how the change represented by this substitution is grounded in the fall.

is essential to the extraordinary ministry with which she has been clothed, woman ought to remain woman, according to Saint Paul, and, though inspired to warn man, she should recall that she is man's glory and withdraw from the world's gaze.

## THE EFFECTS OF THE FALL

Such being the order of creation, it remains for us to know whether woman's primitive mission has been changed by the fall of our race, which has so profoundly disrupted the work of God.

## THE RESULTS OF SATAN'S SEDUCTION

Satan begins by seducing the woman,[10] after which he uses her to seduce the man. This course is doubly clever in that he is more certain to succeed with the woman, because she is weaker than the man, and more certain to succeed with the man, because the woman has greater influence over him than he has over her. Yet was this sweet influence lent to her in order to overrule the man's conscience, to be a stumbling block for him rather than a help, and to give him sin and death in exchange for the life she drew from him?

God punishes her for her abandoned charity through that supreme suffering without which she will henceforth be

---

[10] It is interesting to read the terms in which Pierre Lombard sums up the temptation of Eve. "First God had said, 'In the day you eat of that tree, you shall surely die.' Then the woman said, 'Lest we die.' Finally the demon says, 'You will not surely die.' God affirmed, the woman hesitated, the demon denied. She who hesitated drew back from the one who had affirmed and approached the one who was denying." [A.M.] [Pierre Lombard (c. 1100–1160) was a scholastic theologian. This quote, judging from Adolphe Monod's abbreviated notation, was taken from volume 2 of Lombard's *Four Books of Sentences*, which was used as a theology text.]

unable to continue man's race, and he punishes her for her neglected humility by lowering her condition by one level. "Your desire shall be for your husband, and he shall rule over you" (Genesis 3:16).[11] The woman is reduced to waiting on her husband for all that she desires (there is her increased dependence) and to live under his domination (there is her dependence converted into submission).[12]

Do not think, however, that because of this she ceases to be to the man "a helper fit for him." Alas, when has this tender help been more necessary? Such even is God's mercy that the moment in which he humbles woman is also the moment when he confers on her a greater and more beneficial ministry than ever before. It is through a virgin that he will one day give man the desired restorer who is to destroy the works of the devil (1 John 3:8), as if thus to raise woman up again and reestablish the broken equilibrium between the two sexes. And the first name through which he announces his Son to the world is the offspring of the woman. "I will put enmity between you and the woman, and between your offspring and her offspring; he shall bruise your head, and you shall bruise his heel" (Genesis 3:15).

Thus the essentials of the relationships are not altered by the fall. Woman's calling is still that of charity, and her position is still one of humility. Yet everything has taken on a more serious nature. The charity has become more spiritual and the humility is deeper. Embarrassed for herself and anxious to be rehabilitated, woman will no longer live except to repair the evil she has done to man, lavishing on him the

---

[11] Compare this verse with Genesis 4:7, where it appears to be a question of the submission of the younger brother to the elder. [A.M.]

[12] Between the man's punishment and the woman's, we can note a difference that corresponds to the difference we have already pointed out (see page 21) between their respective callings. The punishment of the woman is restricted to the family circle, while that of the man extends over all of nature. [A.M.]

warnings that can prevent the eternal bitterness of sin, along with the consolations that can soften its present bitterness.

## SAINT PAUL'S ADDED COMMENTARY

Here is another commentary borrowed from Saint Paul. "I desire . . . that women should adorn themselves in respectable apparel, with modesty and self-control, not with braided hair and gold or pearls or costly attire, but with what is proper for women who profess godliness—with good works. Let a woman learn quietly with all submissiveness. I do not permit a woman to teach or to exercise authority over a man; rather, she is to remain quiet. For Adam was formed first, then Eve; and Adam was not deceived, but the woman was deceived and became a transgressor. Yet she will be saved through childbearing—if they continue in faith and love and holiness, with self-control" (1 Timothy 2:8–15).[13]

The apostle says here that the woman was the second to be born and the first to sin, providing a double reason for her to remain in modesty, silence, and submission. There, in unequivocal terms, is the place of humility that we just pointed out. But the apostle desires that she make it a place of honor through Christian acts of charity. Good works are the modest adornment that is marvelously suited to her. They are the braided hair, the jewelry, the gems, the attire that give her favor in the eyes of God and man.

But that is not all. Woman will produce man's salvation, even as she reaps her own, "through childbearing," that is by bearing the posterity that was promised to her. One woman

---

[13] Here once again the apostle considers Eve as a type for woman in general. What Genesis says of one woman, he extends to her entire sex. This transition is perceived through the transition from the singular to the plural in verse 15: "She (the woman) will be saved through childbearing— if they (women) continue in faith . . ." [A.M.]

will give this salvation to the world in the fullness of time by giving birth to the Savior, but woman, whoever she is, will give him to the world in her own way by teaching it to know this Savior and to love him. There, once again, is the mission of charity that we have ascribed to woman and that imposes on her the obligation—or, rather, confers on her the privilege—of consecrating herself with redoubled tenderness, not only to the consolation of suffering man, but also to the salvation of sinful man, whose gaze she will turn toward Jesus Christ.

Thus according to Scripture—that is to say, according to God—ever since creation and especially since the fall, woman is a companion given to man to work for his good, and above all for his spiritual good, in an attitude of modesty and submission.

## NATURE SPEAKS ON HUMILITY

Such is Scripture's teaching, and nature gives us the same lessons. The tasks that God reserved for one and the other half of our species are discovered in their dispositions and revealed in their instincts. Very well! Ask yourselves, and tell us why you were born, if it is not for the mission that we just identified for you through God's Word.

## HUMILITY WRITTEN ON YOUR HEARTS

Your place, we have said, is a place of dependence and humility. On this point, Saint Paul does not hesitate to appeal to the innate feelings of his readers, when, after having forbidden woman to pray or prophesy without a covering, he adds, "Judge for yourselves: is it proper for a wife to pray to God with her head uncovered? Does not nature itself teach you that if a man wears long hair it is a disgrace for him, but if a woman has long hair, it is her glory? For her hair is given to her for a covering" (1 Corinthians 11:13–15). These principles seem so incontrovertible to the apostle that they cannot be denied except through an unworthy, quibbling spirit that does not merit consideration. "If anyone is inclined to be contentious, we have no such practice, nor do the churches of God" (1 Corinthians 11:16). Evidently hair, left long or cut off, serves here to characterize a general and profound difference between man and woman.

If "man goes out to his work and to his labor until evening" (Psalm 104:23); if he chooses outside activity as his task, public life for his domain, and the world as his theatre; beyond that, if he exhibits himself before the angels and relates himself to the entire universe—in all of that he cannot carry the name and image of God too far. It is his mission to represent God, not only on earth, but before all creation. For him to resist this sense of an outward calling in order to shut himself up in the narrow confines of the domestic hearth would represent laxness, forgetfulness of who he is, and unfaithfulness to his calling. He might as well put a spindle in his hand and a distaff at his feet.[14]

But things are totally different for woman.

The hearth is her theater, domestic life is her domain, inside activity is her task, and the long hair which the apostle is so pleased to see shrouding her is the emblem of an entire existence that is hidden and silent. It is in the bosom of this existence that the primary obligations of her sex can most faithfully and honorably be accomplished. "Woman," says a great writer of our age, "is a flower that gives off its perfume only in the shade."[15] To hide herself away, to remain peaceful, to keep herself for her own family, to stay at home,

---

[14] The spindle and distaff are for spinning fiber (flax or wool) into thread.
[15] Lamennais [A.M.] [Hugues-Félicité Robert de Lamennais (1782–1854) was a Catholic priest, a writer, and a philosopher.]

and to manage her household—that is her modest ambition (1 Timothy 2:11–15, 5:14, Titus 2:4–5). If the wise man depicts a woman who "is loud and wayward," appearing "now in the street, now in the market . . . her feet do not stay at home" (Proverbs 7:11,12; see also 9:13), you will recall the kind of woman to whom this applies.

Moreover, is not the humble sphere that we assign to woman the very one for which her whole being is predisposed and seemingly fashioned in advance? Her more slender but frailer form, the more rapid beat of her heart, the keener sensitivity of her nerves, the delicacy of her organs, even the daintiness of her features—everything makes of her, in the words of Saint Peter, "the weaker vessel" (1 Peter 3:7) and renders her constitutionally unsuited to permanent and inflexible concerns, to affairs of state, to late nights at the office, and to all that gives renown in the world.

Do not her intellectual faculties hold her equally separate? It has sometimes been asked whether they are equal to those of man. They are neither equal nor unequal; they are different, having been wisely adapted to a different end.

## UNSUITED FOR A MAN'S TASKS

When it comes to a man's work, woman has faculties inferior to those of man; or rather she is not suited for that work.

I speak here of the rule, not of the exceptions. I readily agree that there may be among women certain minds suited to the cares that are, in principle, reserved for the other sex, or that there might be certain situations that would obligate an ordinary woman to fulfill a man's task, if the man is lacking. However, these exceptions must be clearly indicated by God or commanded in the interests of humanity. After all, in woman's mission, humility is only the means; charity is the goal to which all else must be subordinate. And why would

God, who has made such exceptions in sacred history, not equally make them in general history?

Be that as it may, I leave the exceptions to God and to the individual conscience. Jealous to avoid speaking from this pulpit about irritating, personal, or merely doubtful questions, I concern myself here only with the general rule. Within this rule, we see that the broad sweep of politics and science that encompasses the whole world, the bold metaphysical flight and the elevated poetry that go even beyond this world's boundaries to venture into the empty regions of thought and imagination, these things are not the business of woman.[16]

Even language, especially our language, lends credence to this. (And let us not sacrifice this useful remark out of fear of provoking a slight smile.) Language is the simple philosophy of the people, which is often more profound than that of the school. It is ordinary reason's sieve, which, out of the many sayings ventured by the individual spirit, lets pass only those that speak to everyone's good sense. It does not allow woman *to make herself the object of speech*. It applies to her the word *man* with a feminine ending only as an expression of ridicule or blame. Designations taken from public life that give honor to man disparage woman to some degree. To cite only examples that the propriety of this pulpit authorizes, just try to say a *woman scholar*, a *great woman*, a *businesswoman*, a *stateswoman*. One might as well speak of a *cleaning man!*[17]

---

[16] This thought can be seen developed by Kant in *über das Gefühl des Schönen und Erhabenen*, pp 51–55. [A.M.]

[17] This last statement sounds dated to our modern ears. Today's conveniences mean that running a household takes less time than it used to, and a longer lifespan provides more years for work and service after children are grown. Times have changed. New possibilities for women have opened up. Yet the fact that terms such as *stateswoman* no longer sound strange to our ears indicates how much society has changed in 150 years and begs us to consider whether women have pursued what were once

## WELL SUITED TO HER OWN TASKS

On the contrary, however, when it is a matter of the confined circle—confined in extent but vast in influence—where we, along with Scripture, exhort woman to limit her activity, she has faculties greater than those of man; or rather she alone is suited to this circle. This is where she takes her revenge, where she shows herself to be mistress of the domain, and where she uses all those secret resources that I would call admirable if they did not inspire a more tender feeling in me both for her and for God, who endowed her with them.

Woman has a practical glance that seems more accurate the quicker it is, a vision that seems desirous of focusing closer in so as to see more clearly. She has the art of penetrating hearts by subtle paths that are unknown or unworkable for us. She has a comprehensive presence of mind and body on all points at all times, as well as a vigilance that is as strict as it is unnoticed. She has the numerous and complex resources necessary for domestic administration always at hand, an accessibility ever open to all appeals, and a willingness to listen to everyone. She has freedom of thought and action even in the midst of bitter pain and accumulated burdens. She has resilience, or perhaps an unwearying weakness. She has an exquisite delicacy of feeling and a tact that would be so studied if it were not so instinctive. She has perfect faithfulness in even the smallest matters and an able industriousness in doing what she desires with her fingers (Proverbs 31:18). She has the good grace to cheer a sick person, lift up a battered spirit, awaken a sleeping conscience, or reopen a long-closed heart. In sum, God has given her all the secret resources for the many things that we

considered male goals to an extent that jeopardizes their primary mission as women.

cannot discern or accomplish without borrowing her hands or her eyes.

## DEPENDENCE AND RESERVE

Besides, why do we need all of these descriptions when we can appeal to an intimate feeling planted in the depths of your soul by the Creator, a feeling which preceded all your personal reflections, all the warnings by others, and even all the testimonies from God's book? Consider the propriety and modesty to which a woman never stops pretending even when she has stopped keeping it. What are these if not the proof written in your heart and irresistibly transferred to your countenance of the fact that you find your order, rest, and honor in an attitude of dependence and reserve?

Dependence and reserve exert over woman claims that never appear as inalienable as in certain delicate situations where nature seems to play a cruel game by pitting one against the other without either coming to victory. What woman, in an attitude of dependence, has not desired at least once to have the arm of a man to support her and the name of a man to shelter her? But then what woman, in an attitude of reserve, has not held her secret shut up within herself, waiting for someone to come seeking her, even if she must wait until death? Perhaps this death is even hastened by the internal fire by which she would rather be consumed than to let it break out into the open.

This invariable order of marriage, which yields the initiative to the man and does not even allow you the appearance of it, is not a refinement of civilization or even a delicate point from the gospel. It is a law imposed by woman in even the most barbarous ages and among the most savage peoples. No, I am exaggerating. I have a vague memory of having read, in some account of a distant journey, of a tribe being discovered in which it is the woman who takes the first steps.

However, this is a country where the women have descended to the level of beasts and where the men eat one another.

## NATURE SPEAKS ON CHARITY

If nature agrees with revelation that humility is the place that is appropriate for your sex, it is no less in agreement that charity is the task that has fallen to you. Here again, here above all, what is written in the book is confirmed by what is written in woman's heart.

## A LEANING TOWARD LOVE

What is your natural tendency if it is not to love? In saying this, I am careful not to forget that your sex is no more exempt than ours from the egotism that reigns over fallen humanity. But make an effort to think carefully and to draw back into the very depths of your being. Penetrate beyond the ravages caused there by the fall, down to the primitive soil—if you'll pardon the expression—that emerged from God's hands, and tell me if love is not its essence and foundation.

"More superficial than man in everything else, woman is more profound in love," said a Christian thinker. We are also familiar with this touching thought expressed by a woman: "Love is but an episode in the life of man; it is the entire story of the life of woman."[18] She could have gone further and said, "It is her very life."

Just your birth, as it is recounted by Moses, would suffice to give understanding here. The birth of man, formed from the dead dust of the earth, has something more supernatural,

---

[18] Madame de Staël. [A.M.] [This refers to Anne Louise Germaine de Staël-Holstein (1766–1817), the author of novels and essays, who was of Swiss origin but lived in Paris.]

more gripping, more magnificent than that of woman. That of woman, drawn from the throbbing flesh of the sleeping man, has something more alive, more intimate, more tender.

## THE NATURE OF THAT LOVE

But when it comes to love, it is less the degree that matters than the character. Love is the core of your being, but what kind of love? Think about it, and you will find that it is the love best suited to the calling of benevolence that Scripture assigns to you. There are two loves: love that receives and love that gives. The first congratulates itself on the feelings it inspires and the sacrifices it obtains, while the second takes pleasure in the feelings it experiences and the sacrifices it carries out. These two loves can scarcely be separated, and woman knows them both, but do I presume too much on her heart in thinking that the second is dominant with her and that her motto, borrowed from the free love displayed in the Savior's example, is "It is more blessed to give than to receive" (Acts 20:35)?

To be loved—I know it well, my sisters—is the joy of your heart, though perhaps, alas, a joy refused; but to love, to devote yourself through love, is the need of your soul. It is the very law of your existence and a law which none can ever prevent you from obeying.

Man also knows how to love and must love. Just as Saint Paul sums up all of woman's obligations in the idea of submission, "Wives, submit to your husbands" (Colossians 3:19, see also Ephesians 5:22), so he sums up all the obligations that married life imposes on man in the command to love, "Husbands, love your wives" (Ephesians 5:25, Colossians 3:19). Yet what concerns us here is not the ability or the obligation, but the natural tendency. Here we need to recognize that love is less spontaneous, less disinterested in man than in woman.

It is less spontaneous. Man often needs to conquer himself in order to love, whereas woman hardly needs do anything but heed and follow her inward desires. Perhaps that is why Scripture, which several times commands husbands to love, abstains from commanding wives, as if it counted on nature to supply the command. But, above all, man's love is less disinterested. Man loves woman more for himself than for her; woman loves man less for herself than for him. Because man does not suffice for himself, he loves the one who was given to him by God; because woman feels herself to be needed, she loves the one to whom God has given her. If solitude weighs on man, it is because he finds his life to be without charm separated from the helper fit for him; if woman dreads being alone, it is because she finds life to be pointless when she has nobody to help. We may say of her, if you will permit me this comparison because of the serious spirit in which I offer it, "We love her because she first loved us" (see 1 John 4:19).[19]

---

[19] Perhaps someone will say, "If this is the way things are, how is it that the world most commonly designates the sex to which this discourse is addressed with the label *loveable*, rather than *loving*?" The reason is the world's self-centeredness. If woman seems loveable to it, it is above all because she is loving, and the affection that she inspires is born of the affection she has first felt and displayed.

One could raise a more serious objection, taken not from the point of view of the world but from that of Scripture. In many places Scripture points to the relationship between the marriage union and the union of Christ and his church, and it is the man who corresponds to Christ, whose love is essentially active and free, while the woman corresponds to the church, whose love is passive and derivative; so this order should apply also in marriage, where man anticipates woman. To this objection I believe I can reply, "Yes, that is the way things happen externally, but internally things are just the opposite. When it is only a matter of feeling and loving, the woman (whether through tender usurping or deep motivation) really takes the initiative and the active role." [A.M.]

## A MOTHER'S LOVE

Moreover, what sentiment has become, among all peoples and in all languages of the earth, the type of a love that is at once pure, strong, and deep? It is a woman's love, maternal love. Maternal love exhausts life without being able to exhaust itself. It suffers all things, works through the day, and watches through the night, believing that it has been sufficiently rewarded by a caress or a smile. Maternal love is highly celebrated by moralists and poets, yet we believe we can sum up all these praises in just one: paternal love itself agrees to yield to it.

What am I saying? This same love is the one God chose in seeking, among all human affections, a symbol for the love he bears toward his people. "Zion said, 'The LORD has forsaken me; my Lord has forgotten me'" (Isaiah 49:14). One would expect to see "our Father who is in heaven" reply to this doubt that offends him by appealing to a father's love for his child, but no, it is to a mother's love that he appeals. And he names this mother with the name woman, as if to give honor to the treasure deposited in woman's heart through the riches found in a mother's heart. "Can a woman forget her nursing child, that she should have no compassion on the son of her womb? Even these may forget, yet I will not forget you" (Isaiah 49:15).

## LOVE'S COURAGE TO ENDURE

If such is the heart of woman, how can we not recognize in it a soil expressly prepared for the calling of charity that Scripture has marked out for you alongside man? Love not only inspires in woman the desire to pursue the course of devotion; it gives her the courage for it. Yes, courage is exactly the word. At the risk of appearing to propose a paradox,

I will go so far as to say that there is a kind of courage—the kind most necessary for doing good—that your sex pushes farther than ours. I am not speaking of active courage. Here man wins out over you, and should win out. You yield to him without regret the prize of an intrepidness that is ill suited to your sex. A man of spirit could say without wounding the truth, "Women pretend fear the way men pretend courage."[20] No, I am speaking of passive courage, which is required more consistently than active courage in the humble and daily practice of good works. With passive courage, it is woman who offers the finest examples. Man is able to do more; woman is able to endure more. Man is more enterprising; woman is more patient. Man is bolder; woman is stronger.

Do you want to be convinced? Look at her in the pain of pains reserved for her sex, which is also the price of human life. Look at her and compare her with man in conditions of solitude, sickness, poverty, widowhood, oppression, and secret martyrdom. In public martyrdom, man will keep himself in the rank of honor through the grandeur of the theater, but when it is a matter of a martyrdom that is hidden, through prudence or cruelty, in the subterranean dens of the inquisition, be assured that the advantage is on the side of woman.

God knew all this when he apportioned life so that woman commonly has more sorrows and fewer pleasures than man, at least unless you give preeminence to the pleasure of doing good. This pleasure woman savors even in suffering, and through suffering she binds herself to the one for whom she has suffered.

---

[20] Simond [A.M.] [The source of this quote is uncertain, but it is perhaps due to Philibert Simond (1755–1794), an ordained priest who was active in politics and was guillotined in the wake of the French revolution.]

## DOING SPIRITUAL GOOD

With a creature thus formed, who would dare to dispute her calling of renouncement? Her heart had already revealed it to her centuries before a line of Scripture had been given to the world! And don't tell me that at least Scripture is alone in addressing woman about her special obligation to work for man's spiritual good through a holy charity that seeks, above all, God and eternity for him. Even for this admirable thing, nature has made provision—no doubt not enough to supply the warnings of revelation, but enough at least to support them, enough to foreshadow them.

Who does not know that woman's more lively sensitivity, her more open heart, her more tender conscience, her less reasoning spirit, her finer and more delicate temperament make godliness more accessible to her than to man, while at the same time her occupations, which are less abstract, less coherent, less absorbing than ours, allow her more leisure for prayer and more freedom for serving the Lord?[21] Then consider the spiritual mission that everything seems to indicate for her. Who does not also know that the first condition for success in this mission is found far less in the doing, speaking, and direct action to which man is almost exclusively disposed than it is found in the penetrating influence of the example, silence, and self-forgetfulness that characterize the woman who is truly woman?

Yes, we boldly declare that if Scripture isn't correct, if woman wasn't made for a mission of charity in humility, then nature has missed its goal, for then woman has been called to one task and prepared for another.

---

[21] Clearly today the amount of this extra leisure and freedom for pursuing spiritual matters has declined for those women who have taken on many of the occupations and cares once reserved largely for men, but the inherent differences in our nature remain.

## THE NEED TO BE TRANSFORMED

Hear us well, however. It is not to flatter woman that I have climbed into this pulpit; it is to sanctify her. In saying that nature itself has prepared you for the task that Scripture imposes on you, I did not intend to say that you could fulfill it in your natural state.

### BECAUSE OF THE FALL

Through one of those bizarre contradictions that the fall has brought into our race, troubling the work of creation without destroying it, woman is at once both suited and unsuited to her task. She is suited to it because she has certain dispositions that are marvelously adapted to it; unsuited because she has other dispositions that hinder it.

The "enemy has done this" (Matthew 13:28). In the same heart where God's hand deposited the precious seeds of a life conformed to woman's mission, the enemy has slipped in opposing seeds that choke or neutralize the first. But that's not all. With devilish skill, he has gone out, seeking the healthy seeds in woman's heart in order to corrupt them and thus draw harmful fruit from helpful seed.

### BECAUSE OF THE TEMPTER

Yes, the tempter knows how to take those precious resources with which the Creator endowed you for accomplishing your work and distort them to the point where they become obstacles to that work. Under his mysterious and formidable influence, we see your activeness degenerate into anxiety, your vigilance into curiosity, your subtlety into deceit, your perceptiveness into rashness, your quickness into frivolousness, your gracefulness into flirtatiousness, your tastefulness into studied elegance, your versatility into impulsiveness, your aptitude into presumption, your influence into intrigue, your sway into domination, your tenderness into touchiness, your power to love into jealousy, your need to be useful into a thirst to please.

The problem is that the two principal tendencies that we have recognized in woman, humility and charity, have been warped. The same inner nature that sets the narrow circle of family life as her domain also puts her at risk for latching on to the petty side of things, of concentrating her attention on one point. And she can do so with a confidence whose fire is proportional to the narrowness of the field she embraces. Little schooled in doubting things or herself, and impatient with contradiction through failing to understand it any more than she accepts it, she insensibly launches herself with pride along a path that should lead to humility.

Then the same heart-need that prompts her to love and self-sacrifice also puts her at risk of seeking herself even in self-forgetfulness and of carrying renouncement to the level of a requirement, so that she is hardly able to endure something good being done unless she has a hand in it. She is jealous for the man whom she wants to help and please without competition, and envious of the woman who aspires to help and please as she does. This jealousy and envy—note it well—are born of love, but of a love that has been transformed into passion and self-will in the ungodly laboratory of the tempter.

If the essence of holiness is love and the essence of love is sacrifice, then we would willingly believe woman to be superior to man in the spiritual domain. Yet she has applied toward evil those noble instincts that would have made her excel in good. Giving herself over to sin with a fierce and ill-considered abandon that man scarcely knows, she carries vainglory, egotism, greed, intemperance, anger, hatred, cruelty, love of the world, and forgetfulness of God further than he does. It is as if she intended to justify the old adage, "The greater the height, the greater the fall."[22]

Woman's heart is the richest treasure on earth, but if it isn't God's treasure, it becomes the devil's treasure, and one would sometimes be tempted to think that instead of having been given by God to man as his helper, she was formed by the evil one saying, "It is not good that the man should be alone; I will make him a stumbling block fit for him."

## EXAMPLES FROM SCRIPTURE

Do not accuse me of slandering woman. I am not slandering her now any more than I was flattering her a moment ago. I was speaking then and I am still speaking now in line with Scripture. Scripture, which depicts woman's gifts and humble advantages with such kindness, takes up her faults and wanderings with an unusual sharpness that it seems to reserve just for this purpose.

Saint Paul knew of no worse plague for the churches than those women he describes in his first letter to Timothy. "Idlers, going about from house to house, and not only idlers, but also gossips and busybodies, saying what they should not" (1 Timothy 5:13). He is so weary of them that he comes back to them again in his second letter, saying that false teachers "capture weak women, burdened with sins and led astray by various passions, always learning and never able to arrive at a knowledge of the truth" (2 Timothy 3:6–7).

In the same Proverbs that end with a sublime description of the virtuous woman, Solomon brings the force of his bitter and almost satiric eloquence to bear not only on the degraded woman, whose murderous work none has singled

---

[22] I am trying to use a different image to convey the Latin maxim, "*Corruptio optimi pessima*," which I do not know how to translate literally. [A.M.]

out with a more holy horror (young men, meditate on his sayings!) but also on every woman who is unfaithful to the mission she has received from God. He cites the foolish woman who "with her own hands tears [her house] down" (Proverbs 14:1); the irritable wife whose society is worse than "to live in a corner of the housetop" (Proverbs 21:9, 25:24) or "in a desert land" (Proverbs 21:19); the unworthy woman who is to her husband "like rottenness in his bones" (Proverbs 12:4); the hateful woman, whose marriage is one of the four things under which "the earth trembles" (Proverbs 30:21,23); the "beautiful woman without discretion," whose grace is "like a gold ring in a pig's snout" (Proverbs 11:22); the quarrelsome wife, who is "a continual dripping on a rainy day," so that "to restrain her is to restrain the wind or to grasp oil in one's right hand" (Proverbs 27:15–16, 19:13).

Later, having reached old age, this same Solomon gathers up the memories of his entire life and confesses that, as for him, he has searched in vain for a woman after his own heart. "I find something more bitter than death: the woman whose heart is snares and nets, and whose hands are fetters. He who pleases God escapes her, but the sinner is taken by her. . . . My soul has sought repeatedly, but I have not found. One man among a thousand I found, but a woman among all these I have not found" (Ecclesiastes 7:26, 28).

Scripture fills out and confirms these astonishing declarations in its narratives, which all serve as lessons. After explaining to us the entrance of sin into the world through Eve, it explains Lamech, the first polygamist—who thus became the first blasphemer—through his wives Adah and Zillah (Genesis 4:19–24). It explains the corruption of the earth and the flood through the daughters of man seducing the sons of God (Genesis 6:1–7). It explains the temporary troubling of Abraham's faith, love, and peace through Hagar (Genesis 16). It explains Jacob's faithfulness being covered for a long while with a veil through the women of Laban's household (Genesis 29–31). It explains Esau's profane indifference through the Hittite women, Judith and Basemath (Genesis 26:34–35). It explains Potiphar's injustice toward Joseph through the spite of an adulterous wife (Genesis 39). It explains to us the most terrible plagues of Israel in the wilderness through the daughters of Moab (Numbers 25); Israel's laxness and idolatry after the conquest through the daughters of Canaan. It explains through Delilah the shameful humbling of Samson (Judges 16); through the concubine of the Levite from Ephraim, one tribe almost cut off (Judges 19–20); through Bathsheba, David ceasing to be David (2 Samuel 11); through Solomon's foreign wives, his serving their gods, so that from one fall to another he collected the warnings he was later to give to the world (1 Kings 11:1–8). It explains through Jezebel the ungodly, lying, and murdering king Ahab (1 Kings 21:1–16, 25–26); through Athalia, the kings of Judah following the ways of the kings of Israel (2 Chronicles 21:6, 22:2–3); through Herodias, Herod beheading John the Baptist, in spite of himself (Matthew 14:1–11); through Jewish women, Paul and Barnabas persecuted and chased from Antioch (Acts 13:50–51); and through the prophetic woman of the Apocalypse, the whole earth going astray (Revelation 17).

## TO GIVE GLORY TO GOD

This is the holy liberty of the Scriptures, which tell equally both the good and the bad, so as neither to exalt human nature nor to humble it, but to give glory to God who brings about the good and repairs the bad! Woman's heart—so warm but so passionate, so tender but so jealous, so delicate but so touchy, so lively but so hasty, so sensitive but so irritable, so strong but so weak, so good but so evil—this heart must be subdued and transformed so that the sap of life that floods through it, given its proper course, might bring forth in all their fullness flowers of humility and fruits of charity.

## TRANSFORMED BY WHOM?

Subdued and transformed, but by whom? Ah, from whom else could you expect this grace but from the Son of God? Not content with restoring you to your place and revealing your mission through the instrumentation of his inspired servants, he himself came to show you this mission's ideal form in his life and to open the way for you through his cross. Jesus alive, the perfect example of the gentle virtues as of the strong virtues, is the model for woman as he is for man, and Jesus crucified, the only victim who expiates sin, is the only source of that holy love which, varying only in its application, frees both man and woman from sin.

But between woman and man, if Jesus could find readier access on one side than the other, would it not be with woman? He is the one who "is love" (1 John 4:10, 16), who "came not to be served but to serve" (Matthew 20:28), whose being is fully summed up in impoverishment and sacrifice, and finally who appeared on earth only to exercise the highest charity in the deepest humility.

Am I mistaken, my sisters—I leave it up to you—am I mistaken in thinking that there is nothing on earth more pleasing to Jesus Christ than woman's heart? Needless question! No, I am not mistaken; otherwise your heart would have denied all of its instincts! The Christian faith, which is so well founded in the depths of humanity that it is strange only because of being natural, is also so marvelously adapted to all the needs of your moral being that you can be truly woman only on condition of receiving the gospel. The Christian woman is not only the best of women; she is, at the same time, the most woman of women. Oh, you then, who desire to accomplish the humble and benevolent mission of your sex: beneath the cross, or never!

## OFFERING SPIRITUAL HELP

Moreover, my dear sisters, the first help that man has a right to expect from you is spiritual help. Being indebted to you for the consolations of this transitory life is of little importance if he is not also indebted to you, to the extent that it is up to you, for his possession of an eternal life. It is not only true charity—the charity that subordinates time to eternity—that demands it of you; it is justice itself that obligates you to it, as we have shown you from the Scriptures. Your sex has an original wrong against ours that needs to be repaired, and it is a spiritual wrong.

## THE ORIGINAL WRONG

The thing for which we would reproach you in that fall where we only followed you—assuming we don't think we need to reserve our severity for ourselves—is not the death that you introduced into the world, nor is it the life poisoned by endless bitterness, whose weight even your tender sympathy is not always able to ease. It is a greater evil, the only real and absolute evil. It is the sin that the first man was, no doubt, inexcusable in committing but that he was drawn into committing by the first woman.

Imagine Eve kneeling with Adam beside the corpse of one of their sons slain by the other, whom the divine curse is chasing far off onto the silent and deserted earth. There, within sight of the present and visible fruit of sin and at the thought of its future and invisible fruit, if Adam's tender glance does not say to Eve, "Give me back the favor of my God! Give me back my inner peace! Give me back the days of Eden, my sweet innocence, my holy love for the Lord and for you!" do not doubt that Eve says it all to herself. She considers it an inadequate gift to lavish earth's consolations on Adam if she does not also bring him those of heaven.

## REPAIRING THE WRONG

Powerless to undo the evil she has brought on him, Eve urges him, implores him to turn his moist eyes toward the promised deliverer who will repair all things, reestablish all things, and open a second Eden to a fallen but reconciled race—a second Eden that is lovelier than the one whose gate is henceforth guarded by the sword of the cherubim. If such be Eve's feelings, may she be blessed, though she is Eve!

With a heart such as this, Eve approaches Mary, and in the woman who brought ruin to the world through sin, I already see the woman who is to save it through childbirth. Very well, do what Mary was supposed to do. If there is not one of you who hasn't been an Eve for man, let there also be not one of you who is not a Mary and who does not give him the Savior! There, there is your task. And if you do not respond to that task, you will have missed your calling, though you devote your entire life to doing good deeds. Having been hailed by men as a woman of good, a deaconess, a sister of charity, you will be in God's eyes only "a noisy gong or a clanging cymbal" (1 Corinthians 13:1). But how can you give the Savior to others, if you do not possess him in your own heart? Women, hear me one more time: beneath the cross, or never!

## BENEATH THE CROSS

Let us not speak of the holy women of the Old Covenant, who "died in faith" before the coming of the Savior, but not without having "seen [him] and greeted [him] from afar" (Hebrews 11:13). Let us not speak of the pious Sarah, or the modest Rebecca, or the tender Rachel, or the heroic

Deborah (Judges 4:4–5:31), or the humble Ruth, or the sweet wife of Elkanah (1 Samuel 1:1–2:11), or the prudent Abigail (1 Samuel 25), or the intrepid Rizpah (2 Samuel 21:7–11), or the quiet Shunammite (2 Kings 4:8–37). Rather let us restrict ourselves to the women of the New Covenant.

Beneath the cross, Mary, even more touching than beside the cradle, offers herself up without a murmur to the sword that pierces her soul. Uniting herself to the sacrifice of her Son through the most sublime of charities apart from that of this adorable Son, she offers us the type of the Christian woman, who can only help and love while keeping her eyes fixed on "Jesus Christ and him crucified" (1 Corinthians 2:2).

Beneath the cross, Anna the prophetess, classic example of the faithful woman, is one of the first to give glory to the one whom old Simeon has just confessed by the Spirit. In the same temple where she served God "with fasting and prayer night and day" (Luke 2:37), and in spite of her eighty-four years, she rediscovers the energy and animation of youth "to speak of him to all who were waiting for the redemption of Jerusalem" (Luke 2:38).

Beneath the cross, Mary of Bethany, type of the woman intent on the inner life, fervently seeks the one thing necessary and is jealous for the good part. On one day she sits "at the Lord's feet" to feed in silence on the Word of life (Luke 10:38–42). On another day, in the same silence, she anoints "the Lord with ointment and wipes his feet with her hair" (see John 11:2; 12:3), as if she could find no adequate testimony of her respect and love.

Beneath the cross, Martha, her sister, type of the active woman, sometimes lavishes her untiring care on a brother whom she loves, sometimes hastens to a Savior whom she adores, serving him in everyday life, appealing to him in bitter sorrow, and blessing him in the joy of deliverance (Luke 10:38–42; John 11:19–45, 12:1–2).

Beneath the cross, the Canaanite mother, type of the persevering woman, surpasses in faith and light the apostles, whom she troubles with her cries. She triumphs over the silence, refusal, and disdain with which the Lord seems to oppose her invincible plea and extracts from him at last the much-desired healing, along with the most striking tribute any child of Adam ever received from him: "O woman, great is your faith!" (Matthew 15:21–28).

Beneath the cross, Mary Magdalene, freed from seven demons, type of the grateful woman, surpasses the same apostles in love and courage. Staying after them at Calvary and preceding them at the sepulchre, she above everyone else is also chosen to be the first to gaze upon the Lord after he has left the tomb, and she is charged with bearing the good news of his resurrection to those who are to carry it to the world (Luke 8:2; John 20:1–18).

Beneath the cross, Dorcas, "full of good works and acts of charity" (Acts 9:36), type of the charitable woman, after a life totally consecrated to relieving the poor and the widows of Joppa, shows in her death what she was for the church through the void that she leaves and the tears that she causes to flow (Acts 9:36–42). In the same spirit, Phoebe, the deaconess of Cenchreae, "a patron of many and of" the apostle himself (Romans 16:1–2), gives birth in succeeding ages, through her example, to a multitude of Christian deaconesses—it matters little whether they bore that official title before men.

Beneath the cross, Priscilla, type of the servant of Jesus Christ, worked humbly with Aquila, her husband, both in the perils they encountered in order to preserve for the Gentile church their great missionary (Romans 16:3–4) and in the discussions that enlightened and strengthened the faith of the eloquent Apollos (Acts 18:24–28). In the same spirit, Lydia risked disrupting her life by opening her home to the apostles. That home was at once transformed into a church and became the center of evangelistic activity in Philippi and Macedonia (Acts 16:14-15, 40).

What more shall I say? Shall I speak of what, beneath the cross, became of Julia (Romans 16:15) and Lois (2 Timothy 1:5) and Euodia and Syntyche (Philippians 4:2–3) and Mary and Salome (Mark 15:40; 16:1) and Persis and Tryphaena and Tryphosa (Romans 16:12) and so many other women in the gospel, plus so many others who have followed in their footsteps? Shall I speak of Perpetua[23] and Monica[24] and Marie Calame and Elisabeth Fry[25]?

Beneath the cross with Bible in hand—that Bible to which no human creature owes more than she does in either the world's eyes or the Lord's—beneath the cross with Bible in hand is where I like to see woman. It is there, having returned to God, to man, and to herself, that we see her so worthy in her submission, so noble in her humility, so strong in her sweetness. It is there that we see her gathering together all the gifts she has received in order to consecrate them to the service of humanity with an ardor that we men scarcely know how to bear except in passion. It is there that she obliges us to confess that the one who robbed us of our primitive holiness is also the one who offers to us, in the land of exile, the least tarnished image of it.

## FROM PRINCIPLE TO APPLICATION

Oh, you who read our hearts so well, allow me to read yours for a moment. I have said enough on this subject for

---

[23] Perpetua, a noblewoman and nursing mother, was imprisoned and eventually martyred for her faith in the year 203 in Carthage.

[24] Monica (331–387) was the mother of Augustine of Hippo and prayed for many years that he would come to accept the Christian faith. She died not long after seeing those prayers answered.

[25] Marie Calame remains a mystery, but Elizabeth Fry (1780–1845) was a Quaker who worked for both prison and social reform in England.

you—perhaps too much. You accept this mission, but as coming from Jesus' hands. You burn to fulfill it, but beneath Jesus' cross. Come then. In passing from principle to application, I will show you how this mission can be carried out in various situations and how woman, whether daughter or wife or mother, can always be for man "a helper fit for him." You have seen woman's mission, now see her life. This will be the object of a second discourse.

## A WORD TO THE MEN

I ought to stop here today, but I cannot bring myself to descend from this pulpit without asking the men who are listening to me what they think of woman's mission, as I just described it. Many perhaps have had trouble restraining an incredulous smile in hearing me assign to woman a sphere of action that is at once so humble and so elevated, since it calls her to apply, as someone once said, "such great principles to such minor duties." This smile can have two opposite explanations: some judge woman to be beneath the task to which I invite her; others judge her to be above it.

### IS WOMAN BENEATH HER TASK?

There are times and nations before which I would believe myself compelled to combat the first of these impressions and to defend woman's dignity before man. This care would be necessary not only with pagans, ancient or modern, but also with those elevated spirits, those eminent moralists nourished within the bosom of Christianity. To give just one example, Kant, whom no contemporary philosopher has surpassed in depth and energy of moral sense, somewhere reserves the *noble virtues* for man and leaves to woman only the *beautiful virtues*, by which he means an agreeable, spontaneous, effortless, and painless virtue. He says, "Do not speak to woman of duty, of obligation. Do not expect sacrifices or generous victories over self from her. Do you propose, for example, to give up part of your fortune to save a friend? Be careful not to tell your wife about it. Why restrain her cheerful babbling and burden her bosom with a secret too heavy for her?" [26]

What do you have to say, Christian woman? One is led to ponder whether Kant's considerations of woman are much less humiliating for her than the abject state in which paganism holds her. To combat such harsh and magnificent language, it is enough, for want of what man owes to woman, to remind him of what he owes to himself (from whom woman was taken) and to God (who drew her out from him).

## IS WOMAN ABOVE HER TASK?

Nevertheless, in the midst of Christianity, in France, and in the thinking of the day, the excess to be feared is rather in the opposite sense. One would protest on woman's behalf against my doctrine no longer, as was done sixty years ago, in the name of a worn out gallantry, but in the name of the systems and concerns of the day. One would argue that I lower her and sacrifice her in setting out for her such a humble position, rather than putting her on the same level as man; that I err in assigning her a career of such great renouncement, instead of exhorting her to live at last for herself.

No, no. On the contrary, I serve her true glory and her true interests, because I compel her to conform herself to the law of her creation. This is the primary condition for a creature to know complete order and rest. I do not lower and

---

[26] Kant, *über das Gefühl des Schönen und Erhabenen*, p 56. [A.M.] [The English translation given here is obtained from Monod's French, as it seems that Monod is paraphrasing the original German.]

sacrifice woman, who is the glory of man, in inviting her to live for charity in humility beside man any more than I lower and sacrifice man, who is the glory of God, in inviting him to "glorify God in his body, and in his spirit, which are God's" (see 1 Corinthians 6:20 KJV). I do not lower her any more than I would lower and sacrifice the planet in inviting it to remain in the modest path of its orbit, the only guarantee of its safety and harmony.

Yes, there is someone here who lowers and sacrifices woman, but it is the world—sometimes frivolous, sometimes daring—that treacherously takes up her defense against me. You lower and sacrifice her each time that you drag her, whether for the satisfaction of your ego or for the honor of your theories, outside the position that God has made for her and in which we would like to support her. You recently lowered and sacrificed her when, in your novels and salons and plays, you placed her on a pedestal, with man at her feet. In so doing you replaced the mission of aiding and glorifying man with that of softening and feminizing him. Today you are again lowering and sacrificing her when you seek a different emancipation for her than the one she has received from the gospel and when you imprudently claim on her behalf all of man's rights. In place of a mission that she can and should fulfill, you substitute one in which she cannot succeed and to which she is not permitted to lay claim.

But what idea do you then have of woman, if you believe her to be disposed to give up the humble glory of accomplishing the mission to which she is suited in exchange for the humiliating vanity of failing in someone else's mission? Do you really believe she would be content to be an unsuccessful man when she could be an accomplished woman? Do you believe she would willingly lose her natural and legitimate influence in the sterile pursuit of an artificial and usurped influence? Truly, then, nothing more would be left to her but, like a coward, to regret being as God made her and, as if to outwit this ignoble regret, to go and shamelessly beg from our sex a man's ways, a man's name, and a man's clothing. Therefore, do not doubt that I have the heart of woman on my side. If someone might smile in hearing me explain God's mission for her, I can tell you, it is not she. What woman worthy of her name has ever smiled when someone appealed to her spirit of renouncement and sacrifice? It is bread for her hunger; it is water for her thirst. But what am I saying, worthy of her name? Worthy or unworthy, every woman trembles at these pleasant words. The worthy tremble with joy, and the unworthy tremble with bitterness. You yourselves, who turn her aside from the path I trace out for her, admit it; you declare me to be right in the depths of your soul. In spite of all your discourses, you will esteem woman while murmuring against her if she follows my counsel rather than yours, and you will despise her while flattering her if she follows yours rather than mine.

## EVIDENCE OF SCRIPTURE'S VERACITY

Whatever the case, I dare to say that most of those who are listening to me are not content merely to admit the principles that I just developed; they appreciate and admire them. Very well then, let them learn through this example the extent to which Scripture is true. For in the end, what have I done but interrogate Scripture before you?

I confess to you that when I started meditating on woman's mission, I was far from having feelings as strong and precise as I do today on this little-studied matter. I resolved to open Scripture, to listen to it, and to let myself be guided by it, and I was astounded to find there, instead of a few ideas scattered across its forty books and fifteen centuries, rather a complete doctrine, developing itself from book to book and from century to century, passing from the hand of the prophet to the hand of the apostle. It is like a work that a first craftsman only sketched out and then transmitted to another to finish it. It is a doctrine whose wisdom, fullness, clarity, simplicity, and purity, shining in the midst of a profound and universal ignorance, excited within me a surprise that grew along with my meditation. For all of this revealed itself to me by degrees. The place of woman in Scripture, seemingly restrained at first glance, extended itself further and further with each step that I took.

You need to look for woman in Scripture, but once you find her, she appears there clothed with a ministry as beneficial as it is glorious. Even this perspective instructed me. I understood that such as woman is in the book, so she must be in life: great but hidden. I am bold to say that Scripture alone, among all religions and all systems, has known and understood woman. Standing between the opposing tendencies of the southern and Germanic races, of antiquity and the middle ages—one making her man's servant and the other the arbiter of his destiny—Scripture alone has at once spared her "both this excess of honor and this indignity." Finally, through one of those combinations of truth where the world can see only strange contradictions, Scripture alone has made a place for her that is all the more noble for being more humble, and it has held her in silence so as better to clear her name.

## Study Scripture's Treasures

Know then, oh men, know the treasure that you possess in Scripture, and press it with questions so as to steal from it the light it sheds even on subjects it does not obviously intend to illuminate.

Interrogate it, men of thought. Find out whether it preserves, hidden away in its fertile depths waiting for your pride to lower itself enough to ask, new revelations on the

Creator's plans and on the creature's destinies. Find out whether it hides the final solution for some of those problems that are the eternal despair of philosophy.

Interrogate it, men of science. Look at our old earth, which has only had to open its bosom more deeply to more careful studies in order to reveal its perfect harmony with that biblical cosmogony[27] with which it has so confidently been contrasted. Find out whether it has some new secret to say to the genius of a Cuvier[28] in favor of Moses' inspiration.

Interrogate it, men of letters. Look at its sublime outbursts of poetry, its depictions, which are so natural, its narratives, which are so lively, its arguments, which are so simple and yet so strong that our greatest writers glory in imitating them without ever claiming to equal them. Find out whether it might not have some healthy stimulus, some powerful regeneration held in reserve for the literature of our age, which is articulate but also immature, breathless, greedy, impure, and stillborn.

Interrogate it yourselves, you men of state. Find out whether that divine charter, which has served as a model for modern legislation and created European civilization, might not hold hidden in its yet-unopened folds some unknown improvement for our superb century. Find out whether it might, for example, be able to teach our public officials, renowned throughout the world, that the least they can do on behalf of the gospel, which has provided the basis for all freedom, is to leave it free itself.

But if Scripture has so many lessons on matters that scarcely seem to preoccupy it, what will it not have to say to

---

[27] The study of the origins of the universe.

[28] This probably refers to Georges Cuvier (1769–1832), a French naturalist and zoologist who was a major scientific figure of his day, comparing living animals with fossils to understand earth's history better. His younger brother Frédéric Cuvier (1773–1838) was also a zoologist.

us on matters that are for it (and that should be for each of us) "the one thing . . . necessary" (Luke 10:42)? Oh, I entreat you, interrogate it about salvation. Interrogate it about sin and pardon, about life and death, about good and evil, about heaven and hell. Woe to you if your ears are too delicate to hear such language! Yes, interrogate it about heaven and hell, and you will find that the only place where woman can accomplish her mission is also the only one where you yourselves can find grace, peace, and life.

Beneath the cross, beneath the cross, all together, in one spirit and one heart! Beneath the cross to live, beneath the cross to die, beneath the cross to face the judgment of the great day—and happy then to recognize in the one who will be our judge the one who was our Savior!

*second discourse*

# HER LIFE

# HER LIFE

Genesis 2:18

Then the LORD God said, "It is not good that the man should be alone; I will make him a helper fit for him."

## POSITION AND DISPOSITION

My dear sisters,

My first discourse has, I hope, left you convinced that your mission, according to both the Bible and nature, is one of charity through humility beside man and that you have resolved to accomplish this mission in Jesus Christ, who alone can prepare you for it. Are we in agreement on these principles? Then let us move on today to the application. Let us follow woman's mission in woman's life; that is to say, let us see how this common mission can be realized by each of you—assuming you have Christian faith—according to the particular situation in which God has placed you.

## ACCEPTING YOUR SITUATION

I say according to the situation in which God has placed you, and I insist on this point to avoid a dangerous delusion. In hearing me expound woman's duties in a situation different from yours, you will perhaps be tempted to say in a quiet voice, "Ah, if I were placed there, with what devotion I would give myself to loving and helping!"

Believe me, my sister, with still greater devotion, you will not only fulfill your womanly mission in your present situation, you will also recognize that it is, of all situations, the one where you can best fulfill it. Otherwise, why would God, who makes "all things work together for good for those who love" him (Romans 8:28 KJV), have placed you there?

You will perhaps reply to me sadly that it is less God than your own undisciplined will that has determined your present position. All right, I admit that (though I distrust a woman's heart when it is accusing her conscience). You may have come where you are by a pathway that you cannot recall without regret or repentance. Even so, whatever place you are in today is where God wants you today. It is the best possible one for you, if you accept it in a spirit of faith and obedience, as coming from his hand.

With Jesus Christ there is no situation without recourse, any more than there is a soul without hope. The power of the gospel is such that it acts on the whole course of life and constrains an unfortunate past to take its place among those "all things" that work together for the good of those who love God. What matters before God is not your position, it is your disposition, and the surest mark of a well ordered disposition is to accept our current position as chosen by God in the interest of our spiritual growth. That is why I am capturing your moral countenance, such as it is, the way a photograph would capture your natural countenance.

## A Faithful Heart

The man to whom you are supposed to be a helper might be a husband, a son, a father, or simply a man, apart from any individual relationship. Your position relative to him might be one of equality, superiority, inferiority, or independence. It doesn't matter for the goal I have set here. The only thing that matters is that there be in you a true woman's heart, and by this I mean a heart jealous to live, not for yourself, but for another—first, no doubt, for the Lord according to the general mission that you share with us, but then for man, according to the special mission that concerns us in these discourses.

Moreover, Scripture is content to show us the works of the holy women whom it offers as models for their sex, while making no effort at all to explain their social or domestic situation. About such matters we are most often reduced to speculation. It seems that Eunice is a wife and mother, so that she might give the apostle to the Gentiles the most useful of his co-laborers (2 Timothy 1:5). Priscilla seems to be a wife without being a mother, so as to follow her husband from place to place, assisting him in the service of the gospel (Acts 18). Phoebe seems to have been neither wife nor mother, in order to remain free to carry her devotion and service from church to church (Romans 16:1–2). For Dorcas we cannot even form conjectures. All of this is, for Scripture, only of very secondary interest. It is enough that there was within each of them a faithful heart.

The same heart that made Dorcas faithful in Dorcas' position would have made her equally faithful in Phoebe's position or in Priscilla's or in Eunice's, and the same heart that makes you unfaithful in your mission, there where you are, would make you equally unfaithful everywhere else. But "though I speak in this way, yet in your case . . . I feel sure of better things" (see Hebrews 6:9), my beloved sisters, and it is in that firm expectation that I am going to seek with you the way you can be for man—each of you in her own place—"a helper fit for him."

## THE MARRIED WOMAN

I go straight to the heart of my subject, and I take woman in her normal situation, the one in which she found herself as she came forth from God's hands, the one for which she was formed, the one in which she can best accomplish her distinctive task through tender devotion in humble equality: marriage.

### SERVING ONE MAN

That which woman is called to be for man, you, married woman, are called to be for one man.[1] In speaking of your husband, God said, "It is not good that this man should be alone; I will make him a helper fit for him," and you are the one he gave him. If God did not lead you by the hand toward

---

[1] This comment perhaps explains the adjective *own* joined to the word *husband* in the original text of Ephesians 5:22, which has bothered commentators. In Greek, the word *man* designates both man in general and a married man, just as *femme* in French is used equally for woman in general and for a married woman. The husband here is considered by Saint Paul as his wife's *own man*, that is, the one among all men to whom she is exclusively attached by a bond that does not allow for *partage* (*sharing* or *division*). In our language, where the word *mari* (*husband*) already implies that special relationship, the modifier *own* would produce a redundancy. Thus Osterwald in retaining it is more servile than faithful. Martin eliminates it and he is correct. (The same observation applies to 1 Peter 3:3.) [A.M.] [Jean-Frédéric Osterwald was responsible for a 1744 translation of the Bible, which was based on the earlier Geneva Bible and a 1707 revision of it by David Martin. Adolphe Monod most commonly used the Martin version in his sermons.]

your husband, as he led Eve toward Adam, he has done something even better. He has, through the voice of his servants, pronounced over your union a benediction that marks it with a sacred character and, beyond that, makes it a visible sign of the invisible union of the Lord with his church (Ephesians 5:22–33).

Only Holy Scripture would dare to make such a comparison, and only a Christian heart can understand it. Yet to what heights does it not elevate marriage for the one who has understood! With what authority does it not bring down to us the double precept that sums up the husband's obligations so tenderly and the wife's so humbly! "Husbands, love your wives, as Christ loved the church and gave himself up for her" (Ephesians 5:25); "Wives, submit to your own husbands . . . as the church submits to Christ" (Ephesians 5:22, 24)!

Perhaps, alas, the Lord was the last one consulted about the giving of your hand, and this word of blessing slid over your heart on the day it was pronounced. Yet it takes back its divine virtue, revived and seemingly resurrected by your faith today, according to the power that we have just recognized in the gospel to act even on the past. So if you bear the heart of a Christian woman in your marriage today, you can believe yourself to have been just as truly chosen by God for your husband and he for you as Eve was for Adam and Adam for Eve.

As for the husband, I don't know with what faithfulness he fulfills his part of the obligations, but I have no need to know. Whether he fulfills it or not, you are to fulfill yours, for it is to God that we must all give account, not to man, and "each will have to bear his own load" (Galatians 6:5). Besides, your mission is none other than the general mission of woman, applied and seemingly focused in your relations with your husband and, if I dare say so, carried to its highest point through the closest and most personal of all

associations. Take up that position of humility and that calling of charity of which woman's mission is composed and
focus them on one single object. Then you will know what
the married woman must do in order to be for her husband
"a helper fit for him."

## IN WILLING SUBMISSION

Therefore, openly and whole heartedly take up a humble,
dependent, submitted position beside your husband. Is there
some spirit here thoughtless enough to find in these words
food for the inexhaustible mockery this matter inspires in the
world? Then let it be known that I speak in seriousness for
serious women; I speak in holiness for holy women. I don't
believe myself excused from making them hear the pure
doctrine of God through the childish fear of drawing upon
them or myself the ridicule of those who come seeking the
theatre's emotions in the church and come judging the Word
which will judge them on the last day.

Yes, my sisters, whatever the opinions or practice of the
age might be, openly and wholeheartedly take up a humble,
dependent, submitted position beside your husband. It is not
I who ask it of you, it is God who commands it of you. As
Saint Paul wrote to the Ephesians, "Wives, submit to your
own husbands, as to the Lord. For the husband is the head
of the wife even as Christ is the head of the church" (Ephesians 5:22–23). What he had said to the Corinthians about
man with regard to woman, "The head of the woman is the
man" (1 Corinthians 11:3 KJV), he here says about the
husband with regard to his wife. It is the same doctrine, but
noted in its very special application. "As the church submits
to Christ," continues the apostle, "so also wives should submit in everything to their husbands" (Ephesians 5:24). And
later he says, "Let the wife see that she respects her husband"
(Ephesians 5:33).

This submission is for Saint Paul not merely one of the obligations of the married woman; it is her primary obligation, one which contains the seed of all the others. Sometimes, as here, he speaks of it alone. Elsewhere (1 Timothy 2:9–15, Titus 2:4–5, etc.) he gives it first place and subordinates all else to it. Saint Peter uses the same language.

> Likewise, wives, be subject to your own husbands, so that even if some do not obey the word, they may be won without a word by the conduct of their wives—when they see your respectful and pure conduct. Do not let your adorning be external—the braiding of hair, the wearing of gold, or the putting on of clothing—but let your adorning be the hidden person of the heart with the imperishable beauty of a gentle and quiet spirit, which in God's sight is very precious. For this is how the holy women who hoped in God used to adorn themselves, by submitting to their husbands, as Sarah obeyed Abraham, calling him lord. — 1 Peter 3:1–6

Do not doubt it; the harmony, the bliss of domestic life is obtained at the price of each one adhering to his calling. More than one household that promised well went astray only through having confused the tasks that Scripture took care to distinguish. One does not stray with impunity from the divine order. As others take pains to usurp first place, give yourself the same pains to avoid such usurpation, no matter how it disguises itself under clever precautions or tender appearances. May your husband be for you, after God, the center of your existence. As you lose your own name in marriage, may you also gently lose in him your own glory and your own will.[2]

---

[2] Note that the husband comes "after God," so that if a husband tells his

With regard to you, seek to efface yourself, remain silent (1 Timothy 2:12), avoid any appearance of that which hints of arrogance or domination. With regard to him, make it your ambition to obtain praise for him, or rather be his praise yourself, not through an outward radiance, which it is not up to you to give to yourself or to retain, but through an irreproachable conduct, the kind of conduct that all husbands might offer as an example to their wives. Finally, live out in all of its fullness the lovely phrase from Proverbs, "An excellent wife is the crown of her husband" (Proverbs 12:4).

## IN ACTIVE LOVE

Quietness is not inaction. Scripture only gives you such a withdrawn place in order to confide in you a task that is all the more beneficial. The special humility that it commends to you with regard to your husband is evidence of the special charity with which you will devote yourself to his happiness.

The apostle, who is pleased to see you remain modestly in the home, wants you, through your tenderness, prudence, good management, and care of your children, to make that home into a sanctuary of order, peace, and well-being. There, after the activity of the outside world and the cares of business, your husband can find his chosen rest and his favorite diversion (see Titus 2:4–5, 1 Timothy 5:14). May he find it so well at home, beside you, that he would have no thought of seeking elsewhere for the contentment he needs to dispel his fatigue, lighten his difficulties, calm his agitated spirits, and restore their lost elasticity.

May he even find there—for I refuse you no manner of being useful to him—may he find, hidden in the bosom of

---

wife to do something obviously contrary to God's Word, she must obey the Word.

the domestic hearth, wise counsel and healthy inspirations that will silently follow him into public life and will do their part toward controlling the words on his lips and the decisions in his hands through motives higher than the passions and impulses of most others.

Finally, may he find there all that could make him happy inside, along with all that could make him useful outside. In crossing the threshold of his home to reengage in his noble labors, may he whisper in gratitude toward you and toward the God who gave you to him Solomon's touching maxim, "House and wealth are inherited from fathers, but a prudent wife is from the LORD" (Proverbs 19:14). Happy are you if you can hear it come from his mouth! But no, that isn't necessary. Your sense of awareness will tell you what he is thinking on the subject. As he is touched with emotion, reviewing in his mind all the good things he has received from God—fortune, health, family—it will tell you whether you are the first and last of his earthly treasures, the one he fears most to lose.

## NOT IN IDOLATRY

Nevertheless, let your devotion not be idolatry. Love and be loved in God. The most intimate of all relations ought also to be the most holy, and the gospel would never have seen marriage as a type of Christ and the church if it had not first sought there a sanctifying influence exerted by each spouse on the other. "Wife, how do you know whether you will save your husband? Husband, how do you know whether you will save your wife?" (1 Corinthians 7:16). These serious words set forth the great obligation of marriage, which is especially—for reasons explained in my first discourse—the obligation of the wife, whom the apostle here names first.

God has placed this tender, penetrating—I almost said irresistible—influence in your hands. Woe to you if you know the art of applying it to everything except its true use, the glory of God and the salvation of your husband!

Do you have the privilege of being united to a true disciple of Jesus Christ? Your task is then so sweet that I scarcely need to urge you to be for him a constant source of edification, never a stumbling block. A faithful wife sustaining the heart and strengthening the hands of a faithful husband for life's battles truly is "a helper fit for him" in all her glory.

## As a Faithful Witness

Nevertheless, I want to suppose that your husband, if not a stranger to the faith, is at least wavering between it and the unbelief of his natural heart, distracted as he is by business concerns, drawn astray by the temptations of public life, and, moreover, dominated by a skeptical and difficult spirit. Perhaps all that is needed to protect him from so many stumbling blocks and win him forever to the faith is to see it in action with his own eyes so close to him that he can neither misjudge the reality of the actions nor be suspicious of the sincerity of the feelings.

Do you not recognize there your unique calling? Who besides you could provide such a practical, near-at-hand, incontestable "demonstration of the Spirit and of power" (1 Corinthians 2:4), which alone can bring light to his soul? That is exactly the kind of persuasion for which you have been prepared by God, and no one else can take your place in providing it. Unlike man, woman does not have the mission of preaching the Savior and revealing him; she does less, yet more. She gives birth to him through the power of the Holy Spirit.[3] She gives him, all of him, fully alive.

---

[3] I borrow this thought from a passage that the reader will give me the pleasure of presenting in its entirety:

Rather than proclaiming him through idea and word, she communicates him through deed and feeling and, if I may say so, by way of inspiration. Thus it is reserved for her not to teach the gospel to her husband but to imply it to him through her works, through her everyday speech, through the

---

"The mission of women has always been high in the preaching of Christianity. This was prefigured already in its beginnings in the person of the holy friends of the Virgin, who, having preceded even the beloved disciple at the Savior's tomb, were the first to know of the resurrection, announcing it to the apostles. The mission of women is, in general, less to explain the truth than to make it felt. Mary does not reveal the divine Word, but she gives birth to him through the power of the Holy Spirit.

"Here again one finds a type of the ministry of man and the ministry of woman in proclaiming the truth, which is only its perpetual annunciation. In order for the truth to take hold of us, it must first be revealed to our understanding. That is man's special function, because the rational faculty dominates in him. As reason, "which enlightens everyone . . . coming into the world" (John 1:9), is that which depends least on the inner differences that distinguish each individual, and as it is the fundamental, ordinary, obvious bond in human society, man's ministry in teaching the truth is a public ministry, addressed to the masses. His is the pulpit, the preaching in the church, the adjudication of doctrine. What predominates in woman is emotional power or feeling. This predominance of feeling determines the mission appropriate for women. Its goal is to make the truth pass into the heart, to convert it into love. But feeling is not taught, it is implied. Love in man, as in God himself, is not born through revelation; it proceeds through inspiration, and inspiration depends on that which is most intimate within the soul that is to be brought to love the truth. Inspiration depends on those infinitely delicate nuances, on those thousand almost imperceptible circumstances, on that invisible network of emotions, memories, dreams, and hopes that distinguish one heart from another.

"The great voice that proclaims the truth across the centuries is composed of two voices. To man's voice belongs the loud, dominant sounds, while it is woman who breathes out the minor, veiled, rich tones whose silence would leave to the other voice only the harshness of force. Their union results in majestic, sweet harmony." (Gerbet, *Mission des femmes*) [A.M.] [This is probably Olympe-Philippe Gerbet (1798–1864), a Catholic bishop and writer in France.]

pure, clear depth of her being, and through the whole course of domestic life. She will cause him to find the gospel everywhere without pretending to put it anywhere.

If we count on you, Christian women, for this precious influence, if we see in you the most useful adjunct to our preaching, then we have received the example urged by Saint Peter, whose thought I am, at the moment, only developing. As we have seen, he advises, "Wives, be subject to your own husbands," but why? "So that even if some do not obey the word, they may be won without a word by the conduct of their wives—when they see [literally, *watch* or *spy out*] your respectful and pure conduct" (1 Peter 3:1–2). How could we elevate the spiritual worth of the Christian woman any higher? She even complements the action of the divine Word in her husband's life when her conduct, watched in the setting of intimate conjugal life, allows nothing to be seen in her but the secret virtue with which the gospel works in her heart. A man would have to be truly blind and hardened not to yield, in the long run, to the daily sight of living and true godliness on the part of his wife. The fruits which he gathers are so sweet that one wonders who gains the most, he for the present life or she for eternity.

Whatever the case, woman, be faithful and wait on God's faithfulness. You would envy the wife who hears her husband saying to himself, "a prudent wife is from the LORD" (Proverbs 19:14), but what do you think is going on in the heart of that other woman who, one day as she is involuntarily hidden, hears her husband fall to his knees and cry out, "My God, I bless you for having given me a faithful wife who led me to you"? This testimony will perhaps be refused to you on earth, but how many men give it today over the tomb of a wife whom they will forever seek in a better dwelling place! How many men, at the last day, when all veils are lifted, will say before their judge, in the deepest sense of the words, "It is good that I was not alone"!

## THE EXCELLENT WIFE

Would you like to see all that I have just said and all that could still be said on this subject summed up in a few lines? Read the description of the excellent wife as it is set out by an inspired pen, and this pen belongs to a woman directing her son in the choice of a spouse. If the general tone or a few isolated points of this picture seem in contrast to the portrait of the Christian wife in the gospel, do not forget that it is taken from the Old Testament, where the brightness of the visible things serves as an emblem of invisible and spiritual beauties.

An excellent wife who can find?
    She is far more precious than jewels.
The heart of her husband trusts in her,
    and he will have no lack of gain.
She does him good, and not harm,
    all the days of her life.
She seeks wool and flax,
    and works with willing hands.
She is like the ships of the merchant;
    she brings her food from afar.
She rises while it is yet night
    and provides food for her household
    and portions for her maidens.
She considers a field and buys it;
    with the fruit of her hands she plants a vineyard.
She dresses herself with strength
    and makes her arms strong.
She perceives that her merchandise is profitable.
    Her lamp does not go out at night.
She puts her hands to the distaff,
    and her hands hold the spindle.

She opens her hand to the poor
    and reaches out her hands to the needy.
She is not afraid of snow for her household,
    for all her household are clothed in scarlet.
She makes bed coverings for herself;
    her clothing is fine linen and purple.
Her husband is known in the gates
    when he sits among the elders of the land.[4]
She makes linen garments and sells them;
    she delivers sashes to the merchant.
Strength and dignity are her clothing,
    and she laughs at the time to come.
She opens her mouth with wisdom,
    and the teaching of kindness is on her tongue.
She looks well to the ways of her household
    and does not eat the bread of idleness.
Her children rise up and call her blessed;
    her husband also, and he praises her:
"Many women have done excellently,
    but you surpass them all."
Charm is deceitful, and beauty is vain,
    but a woman who fears the LORD is to be
        praised.
Give her of the fruit of her hands,
    and let her works praise her in the gates.
                  —Proverbs 31:10–31

---

[4] This verse provides an admirable application of Proverbs 22:4: "The reward for humility and fear of the LORD is riches and honor and life." What then is the share due to the virtuous wife if her husband owes her even the renown he enjoys in public life? [A.M.]

## NOT THE SELF-SEEKING WIFE

A wife without humility, rather than being the glory of her husband, seeks only a means to glorify herself through her union with him. She is pleased to eclipse the only one whom she should allow to be seen and finds less charm in his approving smile than in the flattery of strangers.

A wife without charity abandons to hired hands the primary interests of her house and even the care of her children. She gives her husband the example of seeking her pleasures away from home. She contradicts him with bitterness and sourly raises his real or imagined faults. Uneasy and sullen at home, she is gracious and considerate as soon as she has crossed the threshold. She is a wife without godliness, ready to say of her husband, as Cain said of Abel, "Am I his keeper?" (Genesis 4:8). Or she may use her influence only to turn him from the Lord, as did Joram's wife, whose deadly influence the Holy Spirit depicts in the single phrase, "He [Joram] walked in the way of the kings of Israel, as the house of Ahab had done, for the daughter of Ahab was his wife" (2 Chronicles 21:6).

Such a wife forces her husband to secretly groan over the day when he was blind enough to seek her hand, even as he waits to spell out before God's tribunal the full extent of the evil she has done to him for eternity.

Oh, you who recognize traits of your own image in this picture, what shall I say to you? Change, in order to become a woman after God's heart and after man's heart! Change; you can still do it. You need neither youth nor beauty nor an elevated spirit; you need only to become a Christian wife!

## THE YOUNG DAUGHTER[5]

Because woman today does not, like Eve, enter into marriage at birth, let us now consider her at the point in her development where she begins to prepare herself for her future task, and let us address the young daughter. Understand well, my young sister, what it is that characterizes your situation and its privilege. The course to follow is still all in front of you. While those who have preceded you cannot look back without having much to deplore, to repair, and, if possible, to erase, nothing stops you from reserving all the time, resources, and life that you have for your mission as a woman, under God's blessing.

### UNDER GOD'S BLESSING

I said under God's blessing, for what good are the most sincere resolutions without him, especially the resolutions of a young daughter? Nowhere is the spirit more willing and the flesh weaker (Matthew 26:41). The wind plays no more capriciously with sand than the tempter plays with the plans for faithfulness that you form for the future. Alas, they are like the plans formed by so many women at your age, women whose lives today correspond so little to your ideal and still less to theirs!

Far be it from me, my dear daughter, to discourage your generous promises. I only want you to carry them to the foot of the cross, so that you may shelter your weakness beneath the strength of almighty God. Then, I will give myself over

---

[5] The French *jeune fille* can be translated as *girl*, *young daughter*, or *young woman* (the latter is more commonly *jeune femme*, as later in this section). Earlier translators have differed here. However, the context shows that Monod is addressing someone old enough to be preparing for adult life, yet too young to be married and thus still living in her parents' home.

without fear to the pleasure of contemplating in you the living type of hope. Hope is that incomparable grace of all that is young but raised still higher in a young woman, through her greater influence and through her more unknown destiny. Besides, who has ever conceived of personifying hope other than through the traits of a young daughter?

## THE MISSION TO PREPARE FOR

In this uncertain expectation, the question is whether the young daughter should be prepared for the general mission of humanity or for the special mission of a wife. Authors who have discussed the education of daughters are divided on this point. Let us say, based on the Scriptures, that both answers are incomplete.

Yes, no doubt, the young daughter needs to be prepared for the general mission of humanity, which is to glorify on this earth the God who made us in his image, but that preparation is not enough. For, independent of the general mission that she shares with man, woman also has a special mission, the one that concerns us in these discourses.

Yes again, the young daughter needs to be prepared for the special mission of a wife, which is to be "a helper fit for him" toward a specific man, for in the normal course of things the young daughter marries. Yet that preparation should not be exclusive, for not every woman is called to marriage, and an education oriented uniquely in that direction risks missing the mark.

Here is the secret to bringing it all together. Between the general mission of humanity and the special mission of a wife, there is for woman a third mission, special with respect to the first and general with respect to the second. Peculiar to woman and common to all women, it is the one I explained from the Scriptures, where Moses reveals it in calling woman

"a helper for man" (see Genesis 2:18) and Saint Paul reveals
it in calling her "the glory of man" (1 Corinthian 11:7). It
is for that mission that I want to see a young daughter prepared, yet without losing sight either of the supreme necessity of glorifying God or of the natural possibility of marriage.
Provision for both of these will be made through the inter-
mediate preparation we advocate, if it is what it should be.

## THE SPIRIT OF THE PREPARATION

May young daughters keep watch over the spirit of this
preparation, and may their mothers keep watch for them.
Since the quality of greatest worth in a woman, after fear of
God, lies in the humble virtues of domestic life, the principal care of a daughter, after those that she gives to her soul,
should be the formation of those inner, hidden virtues.

It is scarcely necessary for me to say to a young daughter, " 'Abstain from every form of evil' (1 Thessalonians
5:22); keep yourself well removed from pastimes, shows,
or readings—think carefully, readings—that would carry the
least threat to the purity of your heart." But it will, perhaps, be less superfluous to say to her, "Do not trust the
maxims of an egotistical and carnal age." Seeking in the
young daughter only a pleasant plaything to outwit the
boredom that devours it, the age hastily decks her out in the
showy graces, rather than slowly adorning her in the useful
graces.

A vain glamour, a precocious development, misdirected
knowledge, a memory burdened with no concern for understanding, gifts of imagination given preeminence—there is
the showy tinsel that today's education prefers for our daughters in place of the pure gold of a solid, beneficial instruction
which is precious before God and men. I have no difficulty
believing, my dear sisters, that the tinsel would be for the age,
whereas the pure gold will be for you and your home.

I do not mean to exclude you from any serious study, because I do not want to forbid you any legitimate means of influence. Give yourself without qualms to that cultivation of the imagination, literature, or art which, while developing an essential and too often neglected side of the human spirit, also aids the healthy influence that you desire to exert by giving you added ways to please. Only put each thing in its place, and arrange the objects of your study in the interest of your mission. Before all else, be yourselves, be women, and never sacrifice to the false tastes of men the distinctive occupations of your sex. Don't speak to me of a daughter who can garner all of the applause in a concert and does not know how to hold a needle or make herself useful in a home.

Moreover, I can sum up all my exhortations on this point in just one: Let the heart be well regulated and it will take up the task of regulating the life. Humility and charity are the appropriate graces for a woman and the primary conditions for her mission, so cultivate them within you through the Word of God and through prayer. Even without the gospel and your own conscience, the world itself would teach you that if humility and charity were banished from the earth, they would find their last refuge in the heart of the young Christian daughter.

## BENEATH THE CROSS

As for me, if I love to see woman beneath the cross with Bible in hand, it is the young daughter above all whom it pleases me to contemplate there, preparing herself for her future career. This career, whatever it might be, is known only to God and could only be faithfully provided beneath the cross with Bible in hand.

One more word for you and your families, a word given without development and dealing with a matter as serious as it is delicate. Let it be clear that you have unshakably determined to give yourself "only in the Lord" (1 Corinthians 7:39). You will place your hand only in that of a man who is moral, religious, and able to enter with you into the Christian concept of marriage (Ephesians 5:19–33). With that completely passive resolution, not only would ill-suited marriages be avoided, but such a salutary influence would be exerted on the mores and principles of society that man would have found in modest daughters the most useful "helpers fit for him," not to mention the most powerful of reformers!

## HELPING YOUR BROTHER

Nonetheless, you have no need to wait for that uncertain future in order to be to man "a helper fit for him." You can begin now; not to mention that accomplishing your present task is the best guarantee for accomplishing your future task.

Your current position demands a special reserve on your part, it's true. The humble equality of the wife is one thing; the respectful inferiority of a daughter who has only just begun to cross the threshold out of childhood is something quite different. Yet that reserve permits, it even favors a kind of useful activity that is appropriate for your age. True humility supports true charity. The fragrance of the flowers that hide their tender colors beneath the grass is no less sweet than that of others. How much good you can do without ever leaving the paternal home!

You have a school and a parish ready-made in those young children in the family whose education you already share with their mother. Contrary to the common rule of prophets (see Matthew 13:57), it is "in your hometown and in your own household" that God calls you to exercise your humble ministry. Understand what you can do for this young brother, before whom your several-year advantage gives you special credit and whose trust is all the freer because it is not constrained by respect.

You can be like that tender sister watching over the floating cradle consigned to the Nile when prudence does not allow a mother to show herself. Thanks to her youth, she is used, without giving rise to offense, to give Moses a faithful mother as his nurse at the very moment that God gives him an unfaithful princess as his mother (Exodus 2:1–10). Then she disappears from the scene, content at having pushed into the world a brother whose name must one day erase her own. In the same way, God has placed you beside your brother in order to lend him such support as he would perhaps not find anywhere else or which would at least be more suspect. Yesterday you were teaching him to read or write, today you are setting him aflame with unwearying ardor in his wearisome studies, tomorrow you will be advising him in the choice of a career or a wife.

## SERVING YOUR PARENTS

But those for whom you can do the most are the very ones from whom, after God, you have received everything. In the life of a father and mother, who could replace this daughter who is timid and silent with strangers yet full of both sweetness and fire at home—such being nature's marvelous combinations at this age? Who will replace her light and caressing hand, her quick and penetrating spirit, her tender and submissive affection, her simple yet firm godliness? Who will replace all of that in lightening the weight of years, easing their pains, dispelling their worries, anticipating their desires, rejoicing their hearts, and edifying their souls? It is as if she were jealous to give back to them in double measure the life she has received from them.

This young daughter whom you see hiding behind her mother, blushing at the glances she receives in spite of herself, do you not see what she is? She is more than the ornament of the home. She is its joy, its life, its support. Or, if you prefer an expression borrowed from Scripture, she is its corner pillar. "May our sons in their youth be like plants full grown, our daughters like corner pillars cut for the structure of a palace" (Psalm 144:12). And you know the full meaning in Scripture—so exact even in its boldest poetry—of the name corner pillar or cornerstone (Psalm 118:22, Matthew 21:42, Ephesians 2:20).[6]

Alas, one day you will, perhaps, understand the deep truth of this image on seeing the void created in the home when this timid child has just been removed from her place by death! Then you will understand all that her love, her devotion, her godliness were for those who surrounded her and who weep for her. But no, you won't understand it. Only those within the home will understand. Let us withdraw. Even sympathy can be troublesome. Let those of us who have never entered into the secret of their joy not meddle in the secret of their sorrow!

## Ministering Outside the Home

That is not all. There are good works for which I permit the young daughter to leave the sanctuary of the home and, if need be, even the very reserve that her age prescribes for her. Is it a matter of teaching the ignorant, relieving the poor, encouraging the sick, "visiting orphans and widows" (see

---

[6] The French text of Psalm 144 that Adolphe Monod quotes uses the term *pierre angulaire*, or cornerstone, which is the term the King James Version in English uses, while the ESV has "corner pillar." In Psalm 118 and in Matthew 21 and Ephesians 2, *cornerstone* is used consistently in both the French and in the ESV. Interestingly, the Hebrew of Psalm 118 and the Greek of Matthew 21 have what is more literally "the head of the corner," a less definite term. What is clearly in view here, in any case, is a support for the structure (Kingdom of God, when referring to Christ, or the family home, when referring to the daughter) that is both strategic and of highest quality.

James 1:27)? Go, my daughter, go without hesitating, and may the Lord go with you!

When a young daughter has just assisted her mother with the household chores, lent her arm to her elderly father, or read the Bible with her brothers and sisters, I love to see her pass from this charity within the home to charity outside of it. I love to see her carry her care to the unfortunate, who receive it from her with double gratitude, surprised to see her reserve for such a use the same graces that so many others feel free to devote to the world and its pleasures! Free? So be it, if one wants, but permitted or not, the life of pleasure would doubtless seem less desirable to you, less in keeping with woman's mission, than the life I just proposed for you.

Or would you, on the other hand, more readily recognize the "helper fit for him" in the young daughter who prefers the shameful honors of Herodias' daughter to the modest glory of Rebecca; who prefers to be the idol of the salons rather than the treasure of the family; who finds it more agreeable to labor in burdening herself with outward adornments than to be herself the adornment of her home, as God made her to be? Would you more readily recognize the "helper fit for him" in the one who consumes herself with efforts to attract men's gaze and surpass her companions—I should have said her rivals (and don't accuse me of exaggeration)—or the one who delivers to the winds, who tosses into the void the abundant sap of life that was given to her for a day and which tomorrow she will seek and no longer find? Poor child, she resigns herself to being buried alive in the cold joys of the age (1 Timothy 5:6), a sad victim offered day by day, night by night, to the frivolousness of the world through the vanity of her own heart.

One morning at daybreak, two young daughters meet suddenly in the silent street. One is leaving the ball and runs to her bed where she hastens to rest from her pleasures; the other leaves her bed to hurry to a dying person who has just called for her in haste, being, as he says, unable to depart in peace without his good angel beside him.

Young daughters, choose!

## THE MOTHER

We have just contemplated woman before marriage. Now let us contemplate her after marriage, charged with the precious fruit that Scripture calls "a heritage from the LORD" (Psalm 127:3). Let us turn to the wife who has become a mother.

### SERVING IN A PLACE OF SUPERIORITY

Christian mother, beside this son whom God has just given you, you occupy a place not of inferiority as a daughter, nor of equality as a spouse, but of superiority. Yet that superiority does not exclude the renouncement appropriate for woman's mission. It is not good that the child should be alone, and God, who has given him to you, has at the same time given you to him as "a helper fit for him."

There is none among the tender cares that his physical development requires of you that will not be dear to your heart. Jealous to nourish him with your own life, as if to prolong the pride of having given him being, you will not, without absolute necessity, deprive him of the treasures with which nature has enriched you through him and for him, nor would you deprive yourself of the holy pleasure of being undividedly a mother.

### HIS EDUCATION

Nonetheless, I have, at the moment, a more serious concern. The help that you owe above all to this small child is education—the birth of his spirit, which follows right along

with that of his body and over which nobody can dispute
your claim.

You are not like those mothers who see less "a heritage"
than a sign of wrath in their fertility, who were calculating
the sacrifices that a child could cost them long before his
birth, and who need belated experience to learn not to hate
him. Was the inexpressible joy with which you greeted this
son anything other than the natural joy of Eve, who called
her firstborn Cain, or *gotten*, for "I have gotten a man with
the help of the LORD" (Genesis 4:1)? Or is it a more noble
joy, assumed by Jesus Christ in the words whose vibrant
truth has so often made you tremble: "When a woman is
giving birth, she has sorrow because her hour has come, but
when she has delivered the baby, she no longer remembers
the anguish, for joy that a human being has been born into
the world" (John 16:21)?

Motherhood is a ministry, and the first condition of a
faithful ministry is lack of self-interest. Do not say, "Here is
my very own son, born from me and for me," but say, "Here
is a man born into the world for the good of the world."
Earth, heaven, and hell ask, "What then will this child be?"
(Luke 1:66), as they lean in suspense, with great expectation,
over the cradle of this frail creature whose life has just been
separated from yours. The answer—I say this while setting
aside divine action, which works through human means—the
answer depends, above all, on education,[7] and education depends, above all, on the mother.

## THE EARLY YEARS

It is often noted that the decisive moment in education is
its starting point. The dominant direction that determines the

---

[7] "The one who is the master of education can change the face of the
world." (Leibnitz). [A.M.]

course of an entire life is hidden in those first years. And the first years belong to the mother. Paganism has removed them from her, but Jesus Christ has restored them. Let us not envy her these beginnings. If they are too important for strangers, they are also too delicate and entirely too painstaking for a father. We lack the talent, the freedom of spirit, the time, the patience, but God has given all that to the mother.

None other more surely discerns what is natural for her son—the strengths and weaknesses of his character, the allowance to make for his temperament, the measure of severity or indulgence in keeping with his disposition, the precautions needed to make the most of him without spoiling him.

None other better possesses the art of awakening his curiosity, stimulating his fervor, holding his attention, keeping his eyes open, and initiating him by degrees into the practical knowledge of things. This knowledge, more lively than that of books, also has a greater role in the development of his life.

Finally, none other has the hand that is both gentle enough and strong enough to give the nascent plant that original direction. Too firm for the plant to resist yet, at the same time, too tender for it to want to resist, this hand determines all of its future growth.

## Your Moral Power

The greatest moral power in the world is the one a mother exercises over her young child. Do not ask her for a systematic account of this. She acts through inspiration more than calculation, and she has perhaps never said to herself what I am saying to you. God is with her in the task—that is her secret. Perhaps she seems to guess, but let her do so. She is better at it than you are, and she will do more by guesswork than you will with all your reasoning and scheming. Trust this to God and to maternal instinct.

A contemporary author says, "A general rule—one, at least, to which I have scarcely seen exceptions—is that superior men are all the sons of their mother."[8] Behold that man of firm heart and intrepid voice, whose indomitable courage can in turn brave the prince's anger and control the flow of the masses, and whose firm will—equally invincible to obstacles and fatigue—seems to have undertaken to justify the prideful saying, "Man can do what he wills." Do you perhaps credit his energy to nature? Learn that in childhood he exhibited such an irresolute spirit, such a vacillating character that everyone said, "He will never be a man." It is a woman who made a man of him, and that woman is the same one who brought him into the world.

She alone never despaired of him. Sustained through love, led by instinct, she disentangled hidden virtues from the midst of his weaknesses and worked tenderly, humbly, slowly to bring them to light. She formed perseverance in him through wisely graduated struggles, in which her faithful sympathy desired to share everything except the honor of victory. She revealed him to himself; she gave him back to society. Thus, when on his deathbed this son recalls in his heart the good that he was able to accomplish for his people and his generation, it is to his mother, after God, that he will give the glory. The last name that will be heard to leave his lips, even in his last delirium, is the one he tried to say fifty years earlier in his first babblings.

## THE NEED FOR MATERNAL INSTRUCTION

Permit me to add, without misjudging the value of our institutions, that maternal education is made doubly neces-

---

[8] Michelet, *Du prêtre, de la femme, de la famille*, III^eme partie, chapitre 3. This chapter contains very interesting considerations on a mother's influence. [A.M.] [This refers to Jules Michelet (1798–1874), a French historian. This work was published in 1845.]

sary by the trend of our instruction outside the home. A frequent complaint is that while this instruction places precious resources at the disposal of all classes, it also presents, to say the least, unfortunate deficiencies, both for the heart, with which it is too little concerned, and for the mind, with which it shows itself to be so actively preoccupied.

It nurtures self-love through immoderate use of the principle of emulation and does nothing to instill a holy respect for duty (unless one has learned from it, through a singular abuse of language, to cloth purely literary tasks with this sacred name). Beyond that, what it does with so much skill, effort, and sacrifice for the cultivation of the intellect itself is at best incomplete. The abilities that depend on memory are sharpened through continuous exercise, while those that relate to reflection—even more important than the first—remain relatively unused.

By over-filling the student's every moment, by absorbing too much of his ardor in breathless, anxious preparations, one removes from his spirit the leisure, the energy, and the impulse required to assimilate that which it receives. Thus he gets used to being content with borrowed knowledge, in which his personality does not enter at all, and the development of thought and character is either not done or only poorly done. The flower of originality, as charming as it is vigorous, which nature has refused to no one, falls without ever yielding its fruit. One would say that a merciless standard has been applied to every intellect and that the man disappears into the child, because the child disappears into the schoolboy.[9]

---

[9] M. Depoisier, in a remarkable work on *Public Instruction in the Sardinian States,* indicates the ideal that the education of youth should propose for itself. He says, "The child is made to act according to the principles of his own heart, to distinguish by himself between good and evil, between true and false, in order to prepare himself for battle and to be in some sense the craftsman of his own character, the arbiter of his future destiny. The

The only remedy I know for such a serious ill is in the counterweight of family life and education in the home. These alone can penetrate into the twists and turns of the individual spirit, adapting themselves to its particular tendencies. I count on the mother to save that family life, which is so threatened today by communal life, and I count on her again to undertake the education in the home. Do not be in a hurry to remove her child from her. Let her keep him with her for a long time. Then, when the moment comes for him to enter into contact with public life, may his mother still be allowed to play a role, in order to uphold the rights of the heart, the spirit, and the person—that is to say, of the man.

Are you worried that she is going to exert too feminine an influence? Know that this influence, formidable if it were alone, is an indispensable complement to ours. Man does not have everything needed to form the spirit of man, because this spirit has a feminine element. That is what I call the indefinable something that is tender, penetrating, and instinctive and that grasps or, should I say, guesses the truth,

---

great goal of instruction is thus not to mark the students with the imprint of the professor, but to awaken what is in them. It is not to make them learn to see with his eyes but to teach them to exercise their own. It is not to give them a certain dose of knowledge but to inspire in them a certain universal and fervent love of truth. It is not to conform them to an awkward external uniformity but to touch their intimate, hidden resilience. It is not to overburden the memory but to arouse and strengthen thought. It is not to bind them by deep-rooted prejudices to our individual ideas but to prepare them to judge impartially and conscientiously all that Providence might send their way for them to judge. It is not to expose them to our precepts in the form of arbitrary laws, which have no basis apart from our word and our will, but to develop their conscience, intellect, and moral discernment, so that they will know how to discern and choose that which is just and good in what is presented to them. In a word, the great goal of all teaching is to evoke and strengthen both the intellectual and moral life in the child, because that is the life that we must seek in every being created in the image of God." (*Semeur*, 1846, p 196) [A.M.]

as opposed to the calm reason that takes things into account and the strong will that takes itself into account. In this sense, it has been rightly said that "no man of genius is free of a feminine development." Do not hesitate. Place public instruction under the safeguard of the family, but of the family presided over by the mother. That is the surest means of securing its advantages for your sons while sparing them its perils.

## THE ONE THING NECESSARY

Yet, let us not forget that, in education as in life, "one thing is necessary" (Luke 10:42). That one necessary thing is the mother's triumph. Too often, alas, in the holy task of leading her son to the Savior, she has no one on her side; indeed she is fortunate if she doesn't have the whole world against her. But even if she should be alone against it all, let her take courage. It is here, above all, that God is with her, and God is enough for her.

Is it a matter of a young child? This is her beloved son—but beloved in God[10]—and she, in some sense, holds his soul in her hands. She humbles herself daily with him at the feet of the Lord and instructs him to seek the Lord with his first thoughts and to name him in his first speech. She alone in the world knows the ways she should take to deposit fertile seeds of healthy truth in his soul. They are slipped in with so much love, inserted so deeply, bound so tightly to natural instincts (including the influence of her own image) that neither outer storms nor even inner ones will ever be able to dislodge them. Believe it well, nothing is more irresistible for man or more indestructible within man than the early impressions left by a godly mother and guarded by the vague and naïve charm of childhood memories. A son will twice

---

[10] That is, not possessively but as a gift from God.

doubt the spirit of his father before once doubting the heart of his mother.

Is it a matter of that age where, no longer a child but not yet a man, a son insensibly escapes from his mother's oversight, inspiring in her a new concern? Through faithful use of her past influence, she has gained her son's confidence, and this confidence reassures her today for the future. In those tender outpourings that she knew how to make both a habit and a need for him, she reads even the depths of his heart, and a heart that one reads to its depths is almost a heart over which one is master. Perhaps passion speaks, and he is ready to give in. But he would have to tell his mother—impossible! Or he would have to keep silent before her—even more impossible! And so the temptation is overcome.

Finally the moment comes for a long embrace, prelude to a separation that will perhaps last forever. Christian mother, what do you fear? Your ship has been prepared over so many years in the humble workshop of the family; now launch it (since God so desires), launch your ship in peace onto the uncertain ocean! Follow it with moist eye to the farthest horizon and there, as you see it suspended on one last wave, ready to disappear—disappearing—disappeared—offer your prayer. Commit your treasure to the one who holds the winds and the waves in his hands and who loves even more than you do! You have been faithful to him from the beginning; he will be faithful to you right to the end. Go. He will not forget the promise he seems to have made just for you: "Train up a child in the way he should go; even when he is old he will not depart from it" (Proverbs 22:6).

## MOTHERS OF RELIGIOUS LEADERS

Happy expectations, which a happier experience justifies. If it is true that most distinguished men are the sons of their mothers, it is true above all of religious leaders. Biblical history, church history, and contemporary history agree in attesting to this fact, or—let us rather say—in hinting at it. In order to discover the mother, you have to look for her behind that son whose name has eclipsed hers in men's memory, yet that is what a Christian mother asks. If she has saved her son, she has fulfilled her woman's mission, and if she has saved him without showing herself, she has doubly fulfilled it.

Listen to the Bible. What is the point of the short preface it puts at the beginning of Samuel's life, if it is not to explain this holy man of God, this giant of prayer, this first link in the chain of prophets, this great reformer of the state and of worship in terms of his mother Hannah's faith, her vow, her faithfulness, and her song? Let this account make up for the brevity with which the Bible elsewhere explains Moses (Exodus 2:1–10; Hebrews 11:24), David (Psalm 86:16; Psalm 116:16), and Timothy (Acts 16:1; 2 Timothy 1:5) in a similar way. Let it give us the key to the seemingly minute care with which it names, in passing, the mothers of the kings of Judah (2 Chronicles 22:3, etc.).

Open the annals of the church. Think of Saint Augustine, that bright light twice ready to be extinguished but shielded in turn from covetousness and heresy to glorify the holy and true God before the farthest removed posterity. On hearing his name, who does not recognize in that double deliverance, after the hand of God, the hand of the tender, the humble, the patient Monica? But learn that Chrysostum, Basil the Great, Gregory of Nazienzen,[11] and a great number of those who have followed in their footsteps each had his Monica, about whom we forget to inform ourselves, un-

---

[11] Neander, *Mémoires pour servir à l'histoire du christianisme*, p 247 ff. [A.M.] [The author is most probably August Neander (1789–1850), a church historian who wrote *History of the planting and training of the Christian church by the apostles*, and many other works.]

grateful as we are, while savoring with delight the fruit of
what she sowed.

Yet there is no need to go that far astray. Look around
you. Take the effort to seek out God's ways, and you will
find that most of Jesus Christ's servants in whom our generation glories are indebted to a mother for the first glimmers
of their godliness. At a recent pastors' conference, where one
hundred and twenty American pastors came together in a
common faith, each was invited to make known the human
agent to whom he attributed, under the divine blessing, the
change in his heart. Do you know how many gave that honor
to their mothers? Out of one hundred and twenty, more than
one hundred.

## MOTHERS OF PRODIGAL SONS

Elsewhere, an equally faithful mother seems to have had
less success. Her son has strayed far from the path she traced
out for him. A mother, after all, mother though she is, is not
God. But the greater the straying of that prodigal child, the
more one admires the maternal power to which he closes his
heart without being able to shield his conscience from it.
Who knows? Perhaps this power will finally triumph over his
resistance long after the lessons and examples of his mother
have reached the tomb. To ignore a mother's godliness is
possible, but to forget it—never, no, never.

A good man was making his way toward a church where
a religious service for sailors was going to be held. Across
from the church, at the doorway of an inn, he saw an old
seaman seated. With a rough and determined air, arms
crossed and a cigar in his mouth, he looked with indifference
if not disdain at those of his comrades who were passing by
on their way to the public worship. "My friend," said the
stranger in approaching him, "won't you come with us to the
service?" "Certainly not," the sailor replied brusquely. His air

had made the stranger expect this response, but he continued gently, "You seem to me to have had some bad days. Is your mother still alive?" The seaman raised his head, fixed his eyes on the stranger, and kept silent. "Very well, my friend, if your good mother were here, what advice do you think she would give you?" And the seaman got up, wiping away with the back of his hand a tear that he had tried in vain to hide, and with a choking voice said, "I'll go. . ."

## KNOW YOUR OWN POWER

Mothers, mothers, know your power! Mothers, mothers, sense your responsibility! Fortunate is the child who has a good mother! Fortunate is your son if he has a good mother! But hear us; I do not lavish this name on every mother who fails to hate her child. A devoted mother is one thing, and there are many of them, even among the pagans; a good mother according to God is something else.

In our day, alas, the history of the relations that some men have with their mothers is soon told. All intellectual, moral, and spiritual development is unknown there. From his mother's bosom, the poor child passes into the hands, if not under the roof, of a paid mother. From those hired hands to the paternal home until his age allows him to leave it again. From the paternal home to secondary school; from secondary school to college; from college to the army.[12] When he returns from the army—if he returns—what will this mother be to him except a stranger, since he was scarcely more than a stranger to her before? She will be a stranger to his future career, a stranger to his marriage, a stranger to the education

---

[12] Here "secondary school" is *collège*, but this does not correspond to the English term *college*. At least today, it is for students ages 11 to 15. The term translated "college" is *école supérieur*, which corresponds more closely to American colleges.

of his children. Oh mother who still has a son to raise, wake up! And you, mother, who have raised yours this way, repent!

Yes, repent, but do not despair. The word despair is not Christian. Not only can the worker hired at the last hour be admitted, he can even be favored. You can again become "a helper fit for him" to this son. By God's grace, drawing good from evil, you can experience the truth of the phrase that contains the entire gospel in seed form, "When I am weak, then I am strong" (2 Corinthians 12:10). Where one task ends, another begins. If it is too late for the task of education, you are left with another task, one for which it is never too late since the weight of years imposes it on you.

You no longer reign with authority over children who have become men, but you can still exert over them an influence of love and respect, to which the maturity of their age lends itself. As the last tie between the generation that is dying out and the one that follows, as the fragile and precious remnant of that which was and already is no more, as the watchful repository of family traditions, you form a venerated center around which are grouped in attentive silence many families which your departure will soon disperse. Many thoughts, many interests, perhaps many passions are stirring in the depths of the hearts beside you, but all are restrained by the common feeling that you inspire, and each one competes in efforts and sacrifices to assure the peace of your last days. Your experience, your white hair, your past service, your present infirmity, a vague fear of not finding you in your place tomorrow—all that surrenders their hearts to you.

Noble and useful pulpit, which God has prepared for you! Powerful words received as lessons from life, as warnings from the dead, almost as inspirations from heaven! Happy the mother who finishes faithfully a career that was faithfully carried out! But happy also the mother who, with holy jealousy to finish well that which she began poorly, knows how to turn even her unfaithfulness to the advantage of those who are hers![13]

"Older women likewise are to be reverent in behavior, not slanderers. . . . They are to teach what is good, and so train the young women to love their husbands and children" (Titus 2:3–4). Here in the hidden life is the secret of this beneficial influence: "She who is truly a widow, left all alone, has set her hope on God and continues in supplications and prayers night and day" (1 Timothy 5:5).

## THE SINGLE WOMAN

My dear sisters, either I am wrong or there is a woman here who sensed her heart tightening within her and a furtive tear moistening her eye when faced with the picture I just painted of the Christian wife and the Christian mother. This woman, whether through circumstance or free choice or generous sacrifice or religious faithfulness, has never become a wife and mother.

### A HOLY JEALOUSY

Understand it well; it is a godly jealousy that troubles her in this moment. Exclusively preoccupied with the sublime mission of her sex, she would accept without difficulty that her position has an incompleteness according to opinion, according to the heart, according to the law of providence. What she cannot consent to is having nobody to whom to give herself and carrying in her bosom a thirst for devotion that consumes her without profiting anyone else.

---

[13] According to several commentators, Lemuel would be another name for Solomon in the last chapter of Proverbs. If this is so, then Bathsheba would be a touching example to cite here, since this chapter would come from her hand. [A.M.]

My sister, my noble sister, will the delicacy of the subject close my mouth? It doesn't matter if the subject is delicate, provided I fulfill my mission as a minister of Jesus Christ by helping you accomplish your mission as a woman.

## A PRIVILEGED POSITION

You are, I am happy to say, greatly deluded. Your position, received as from God and in the interest of your mission, is, if rightly understood, a privilege. Here believe the apostle as he was writing to the Corinthians. "The unmarried or betrothed woman is anxious about the things of the Lord, how to be holy in body and spirit. But the married woman is anxious about worldly things, how to please her husband. I say this for your own benefit, not to lay any restraint upon you, but to promote good order and to secure your undivided devotion to the Lord. If anyone thinks that he is not behaving properly toward his virgin, if his passions are strong, and it has to be, let him do as he wishes: let them marry—it is no sin. But whoever is firmly established in his heart, being under no necessity, but having his desire under control, and has determined this in his heart, to keep her as his virgin, he will do well. So then he who marries his virgin does well, and he who refrains from marriage will do even better" (1 Corinthians 7:34–38, literal reading).[14]

These are strange words, we must confess, and ones it would be easy to abuse to the advantage of erroneous opinions on celibacy that were established early in the church. No doubt, Saint Paul's language must be explained by the particular circumstances of the times in which he was writing. Still we may boldly assert that he would never have explained

---

[14] The word "virgin" is the literal Greek in this passage. The version that Monod quotes translates this as *fille*, which often means "daughter" but also can mean "girl." The ESV translates it as "betrothed."

himself in this way if he considered your position as less than that of the married woman for the Lord's service and for the accomplishment of your mission. He had chosen an analogous position for himself, not only to prove to the church his selflessness by not burdening them with supporting him, but also to devote himself "to prayer and to the ministry of the word" (Acts 6:4) with greater freedom—freedom of time, action, spirit, and heart.

These reasons are as valid for you as for the apostle, and the last is of special value for woman. This above all is what I am striving to make you understand.

## Choosing the Right Pathway

There is in woman's heart a power to love to which man cannot attain. In the natural condition, which is married life, that power is exerted and satisfied within the family—on a husband and on children. In singleness it manifests itself in different ways, and throws itself into one of two paths. It can turn inward, folding over onto self, focusing itself in the personality, producing a boundless, unprincipled egotism. It is probably in this class of single women that one finds the most humiliating examples of self-love, curiosity, idleness, greed, worldliness, and a completely petty existence consumed in petty ways on petty pleasures. Or, on the contrary, this power to love can turn outward, pouring itself out in love for the Lord and for neighbors and pushing the woman to devote herself to the good of humanity, just as the wife or the mother devotes herself to that of her family.

Thus, through an apparent contradiction, charity simultaneously gains in both breadth and depth. It gains in breadth because it goes beyond the domestic circle and in depth because it clothes itself with the ardor of personal need and the impetus of personal feeling, not to mention a touch of sweet sadness, which is appropriate for her and which also stimulates her in its way. This is how holy and charitable daughters are formed. Or, shall I say, daughters of holiness and charity, in whom we must perhaps seek the most complete examples of Christian benevolence. Weary of earth and impatient for heaven, they seem to be perpetually occupied with filling up the immense void that God has placed in their heart—and placed there for the good of humanity—through the simplicity of their zeal, the purity of their renouncement, and the abundance of their good works.

Their ranks are open to you. Enter there, following in the steps of so many women who have chosen this position in order to be more useful to the world. Enter there, and give yourself no rest until you have learned to see a merciful privilege in your singleness.

## A PATHWAY OF GOOD WORKS

According to the apostle (Ephesians 2:10), God has a pathway of good works prepared in front of you. All that is required in order for you to walk in it is a truly devoted heart. "Open your eyes, and you will have plenty of bread" (Proverbs 20:13).

First, look around you and see if your family relationships don't offer you the opportunity to which you aspire. Sometimes that which we go seeking to the ends of the earth is right at hand. Lacking a father and mother who have been withdrawn from you, perhaps you have a young brother at the beginning of life for whom you can serve as a friend and mother.

Or perhaps there is a sister, ready to give way under the envied burden of family if she does not find in you the complement of strength, time, health, and light that God has visibly assigned to you for her. Your heart was asking for a family. Very well, there it is. I am well aware that it isn't yours; it isn't all you would like, but it is what God wanted for you, my sister. He is providing for the good of another through your charitable action while providing for your good through your self-renouncement.

No, when I go all over the earth asking for the example of the most useful, the purest, the most Christian charity, nowhere do I find all these conditions better fulfilled than in the good aunt. Through a marvelous self-forgetfulness, she accepts the fatigue and the cares of motherhood without knowing its unspeakable rewards. She is mother, perhaps more than mother, when it is a matter of serving and supporting, yet she effaces herself as soon as it is only a matter of reaping and rejoicing. She is sad but with a heavenly sadness that is fully translated into love and renouncement.

If no family obligation binds you, very well, look further afield. Seek a family in all that has need of you—in those unfortunate ones to relieve, in those charitable institutions to found or sustain, in that faithful minister to help in his labor, in all those good works for which God seems to have expressly reserved your freedom. Or embrace an even vaster field; you can do it. Embrace the world, if you like, provided that it is with charity. Renew in your person the holy office of deaconess. Prepare yourself for it, if need be, in those schools that a vigilant and ingenious charity are opening today for godly girls. Go, new Phoebe, and carry your services now to Rome, now to Cenchrea—that is to say, now to a family, now to a poorhouse,[15] now to the church—everywhere they are asked for, though it be on behalf of some pagan population consigned to live under a different sky.

Finally, fulfill your mission so well that, at the hour of your death, each will be glad for the blessed singleness that allowed you to show such devotion. Then, in the tender regrets that follow your mortal remains to the tomb, one will

---

[15] Literally "hospice," which can be translated as orphans' home, hospice, poorhouse—in other words, a home for those in need of care.

no longer be able to discern whether you were wife or sister, aunt or mother, family or stranger; for it was not evident in your sacrifices!

## THE CHRISTIAN SERVANT

If, rather than taking the thread of my arguments from differences in natural position, I had taken it from differences in social position, I would have been equally able to show you woman—whether in a position of equality, superiority or inferiority—finding special resources for accomplishing the mission of her sex. That matter needs to be left to your personal meditations. Nevertheless, there is one class of women I will not let depart without a few words of encouragement, because I believe it needs them, and I consider it has a right to them.

### THE BLESSING OF DEPENDENCE

Christian daughter whom God has placed in the humble rank of a servant, I hope that the egalitarian spirit of this age, which has a bad effect on all inferior conditions, has not so won you over that you cannot accept the trials of your situation and even appreciate its compensations and advantages.

But perhaps you are saying within yourselves, "This lovely mission of woman is for everyone except for me! What can a poor servant girl do, when she lives dependant on another?" Listen well to my answer. You can accomplish the mission of your sex, I don't say in spite of that dependence, but even through that very dependence.

Many women have strained things in order to create for themselves a path of obedience. They were wrong. They substituted their wisdom for God's. Yet their error comes from a deep instinct in woman, one that God was careful to satisfy in you by choosing for you the last place. That is the place the Savior preferred. He took "the form of a servant"[16] (Philippians 2:7) and came—I love to repeat it—"not to be served but to serve" (Matthew 20:28). Was this an obstacle to his work? Wasn't it rather its support, its condition, and its life? Believe it well, it will be all of that for your work, if you enter into the spirit of your Master.

## YOUR BLESSING TO THE FAMILY

I would hardly be able to name someone who contributes more to the order, prosperity, and happiness of a home than a servant girl who is truly Christian, especially today, when this treasure is so rare and, alas, so imperfectly appreciated when it is found. This holy young woman obeys her "earthly masters with fear and trembling, with a sincere heart, as she would Christ, not by the way of eye-service, as a people-pleaser, but . . . doing the will of God from the heart" (see Ephesians 6:5).

She is careful to please her masters, avoids contradicting them (Titus 2:9–10), espouses their interests, and is scrupulously faithful.[17] She accommodates herself to their weaknesses within the home and—good and noble girl—she covers them outside of it with the veil of her charity. Finally, she raises her condition to the height of her feelings, free through faith and a slave through love. What a gift of God for a family!

You, families, who have received this blessing, be appreciative of it, without waiting for God to reveal its value to you by withdrawing it from you and replacing this godly girl with one of those many servants who are full of the

---

[16] Literally "bondservant" or "slave." [A.M.]

[17] See 1 Peter 2:18 and 1 Timothy 6:1–2. [A.M.]

world and of themselves. Such a servant is ill at ease, as if in prison inside the home, and always plotting with the outside like a traitor in a besieged place. She is scarcely restrained through a surveillance that is more wearying to give than to endure. She is as careful about herself in public as she is neglectful in private and scatters family secrets through the city. She is curious, chattering, difficult, bound by self-interest, and only waiting for the lure of something better to break a yoke that weighs on her.

## YOUR SPIRITUAL INFLUENCE

So much for the present life, but what about the other? Ah, keep yourself from thinking that woman's spiritual mission is forbidden to you. In the humble sphere assigned to you, you can do more than any other for the service of the gospel, provided that you want to serve as a woman, to serve gently, silently, striving above all to "adorn the doctrine of God our Savior" (Titus 2:10) by a conduct that is above reproach.

We have said it before: influence goes up more than it flows down. One who resists the influence of his superiors, against which he is on guard, submits to that of his subordinates, which he does not acknowledge. That was the power of the freedmen in Rome; that is the credit given in Proverbs to the "servant who deals wisely" and "will rule over a son who acts shamefully and will share the inheritance as one of the brothers" (Proverbs 17:2). Spiritual influence follows the same law. Of all influences, it is the one that gains most from being hidden, because it is the one that most frightens natural pride.

Go, your spiritual role is great, and your responsibility is great proportionately. I tell you, there is a kind of retreat that only you can penetrate. There is a kind of conversion that God reserves for you and that none other than you can bring about. There is a kind of proud heart that yielded to neither mother nor wife nor daughter, yet it will be constrained to lay down its arms before the obscure faithfulness of a servant girl. "The last will be first" (Matthew 20:16).

When Peter, having left the prison, knocked at the door of a house where the disciples were gathered, it was reserved for Rhoda, a servant girl, to be the first to run and meet him and to proclaim the news of his deliverance. It is a privilege worthy of envy to open the door for an apostle who knocks; a privilege more worthy of envy when it is the Lord who knocks, and the Lord does not fear those secret doors that only open to him through you.

But the children, above all, the children, the hope of the future—are you considering the sway God has given you over their spirit? How many times has it not been noticed that children, instead of taking the example of their parents, more readily shape their accent, their language, their habits on those of the servants, whether through more frequent contact or through actions which are less obvious and evoke less resistance. Man's heart is made that way. It only remains for you to turn this sway to the benefit of the gospel. In the spiritual development of the child whom you carry in your arms or take for walks, you rival the faithful mother, and you win out over the ordinary mother.

## LET GOD ELEVATE YOUR WORK

With such useful work to do, would you be jealous of the greater works reserved for others? Moreover greatness comes from God, and it is up to him to change the small things that you accomplish into great ones, even in the world's eyes.

When it was needful to bring the powerful and glorious Syrian captain Naaman into contact with the prophet who was to both deliver him from his leprosy and reveal the living God to him, God used a little Israelite girl whom the captain's soldiers had taken prisoner and whom he had given to his wife as a slave. Poor child, she scarcely suspected, when she cried out in the arms of her fierce abductors, that a day would come when she would do such great good to Syria and would be cited as an oracle in the great king's court: "Thus and so spoke the girl from the land of Israel" (2 Kings 5:4). Was it not for your encouragement that this event was reported to us?

Do you know how Illyria received the gospel in the first centuries of the church? Through a Christian woman who had been sold there as a slave.[18]

I say all this not to puff you up nor to be a stumbling block for you, but to excite in you a righteous gratitude and to make you appreciate the position God has given you. Yes, my dear sisters, just conform yourselves to his views. Not a word of complaint or regret, no ambitious dreams of change, but a faithfulness filled with happiness in your own mission and a heart that envies nobody anything except a more active charity and a deeper humility!

## BE A FITTING HELPER

Finally, woman, whoever you are and wherever you are, place in your heart this word: "I will make him a helper fit for him," and without delaying any longer, dream of justifying God's definition of you.

## USELESS WOMAN

Useless woman, you lament at the thought that prior to this day you have burdened the earth like a tree without fruit.

---

[18] Neander, *Mémoires pour servir à l'histoire du christianisme*, p 407. [A.M.] (See footnote 11 of this chapter.)

You lament that you could be removed from it leaving no greater void than does a sword that is plunged into water and then withdrawn. You lament that you have lived until now without knowing where you came from or where you are going. Here, laid bare, is the vague object for which you sighed without knowing what it was. Here is a work to which you will consecrate yourself while alive and of which you will be able to say on dying, "I have accomplished the work that you gave me to do" (see John 17:4).

Even today, according to your situation, whose apparent difficulties are real resources, enter into the life that is so humble and yet so glorious, so sweet and yet so devoted. God destined it for you on the day he said, "I will make him a helper fit for him," and Jesus Christ restored it to you when he "gave himself for us to redeem us . . . and to purify for himself a people for his own possession who are zealous for good works" (Titus 2:14).

## WORLDLY WOMAN

Worldly woman, you have consumed your finest years in cares that are, I hope, innocent but are also frivolous and unworthy of you. Intoxicating and intoxicated, you have taken an influence that God confided to you for his glory and for the good of his people, and you have turned it to the advantage of your own pride. Here, in place of that existence, which shines but shines like a meteor, which resounds but resounds like an empty vessel, here is a glorious and full life, where, in finding yourself, you will at last find the contentment that you have sought in vain—isn't it true?—from the world.

Take your heart back from vanity in order to give it to charity! Believe me, and leave behind that artificial life, which supplants and shortens the true life. Reserve your day's work and your night's rest for your home. Count as lost the days when you failed to do some good. Enjoy at last the happiness of being a woman. Do all of that and you will know that, having been made for man as "a helper fit for him," it is better to be useful to him than to be flattered by him, to serve him than to fascinate him!

## LONELY WOMAN

Lonely woman, from whom God, who "will not answer for any of his own words" (Job 33:13, alternate reading), has taken away the husband of your youth and, along with him, the charm, the goal, the life of your life. And you, rather, deserted woman, the widow of someone living, you are the tender plant that was wrenched from its soil as if to carry it to a better place but then was thrown aside en route and abandoned to the sun's withering fire. The husband of your youth, after a brief time of joy given and received, now waters this plant with bitterness through his coldness if not through his infidelity. You, whom the Lord has chosen in his Word as a standard of the most unspeakable grief,[19] take courage. Your consolation has been found.

If the sweetness of being loved has been stolen from you, do not let yourself be robbed of the privilege of loving, of being the first to love, of being the last to love, of loving always, of loving in spite of all. Follow the path of Jesus, who was neglected as you are but never cold and unjust as someone is with you. Still be for the one who offends you "the helper fit for him." Drink without a murmur the cup that his cruel hand holds out to you each day. Oppose his ingratitude only with renewed submission, devotion, and sacrifice. Keep quiet and humble yourself. Go; this heart that you seek will be returned to you, conquered by your love! But even if he should continue in his injustice right to the end,

---

[19] See Isaiah 54:6, etc. [A.M.]

even if—oh, horrible memory—he should finish his murderous work by one day lifting a menacing hand toward you, yield while still blessing him.[20] Accomplish your mission as woman right to the end. Count on the God whom you love and who loves you to make you share his glory along with his cross!

## FALLEN WOMAN

And you, fallen woman, whom I hesitate to name, charity does not allow me to leave you without a reply, for I hear your heart questioning me.

Let nobody "trouble the woman" (Matthew 26:10). If a sinful woman who repents is a sight not worthy of you, know that it is worthy of the angels! As for me, if I could despise her tears and disdain her repentance, I would not believe myself to be a disciple of the one who said to the penitent sinner, "Your faith has saved you; go in peace" (Luke 7:50).

My sister, my poor sister, yes, this is for you too. Do not believe that you alone are excluded from this call. Be careful not to despair of yourself. Is your heart burning within you to accomplish your mission as woman, to become again for man what God made you to be, "a helper fit for him"? You can do it, yes, you can, and none can do it more than you if none is more thirsty for grace.

Do you know that many of those holy women—Rahab (Hebrews 11:31), Mary Magdalene (Luke 8:2), the repentant sinful woman (Luke 7:37)—who shine in the first ranks among the examples of humanity on earth and among the redeemed of the Lord in heaven began as you did? Very well, end the way they did! Humble among the humble, loving

---

[20] This should not be interpreted as saying that a woman should always remain in a seriously abusive or even dangerous situation. Only prayer and wise pastoral or professional counsel can determine the right course to take in such situations.

among the loving, remember your past only to benefit your future! Do not allow anyone to recall a time that is no more except to admire in your transformation both divine compassion and woman's calling. And may there descend on your head—guilty but covered in my eyes under the blood of Jesus Christ—the blessing of the Father, Son, and Holy Spirit, along with my blessing!

## MAN'S OBLIGATION TO WOMAN

But we, my brothers, witnesses to this new baptism of woman, have we garnered anything from it other than useless entertainment? This concerns our interests, our dearest interests. Yet it also concerns our consciences. If woman owes man the aid of "the helper fit for him," does man owe nothing to woman? If woman has her influence over us, do we not have our influence over her? How faithful have we been to this task of gratitude and reciprocity?

### MAN'S SIN TOWARD WOMAN

I said in my first discourse that sin came to us through woman. Alas, we have returned it to her and returned it with interest. When woman has misjudged her mission, who has made her forget it? When woman has been idolized, who has put her on a shameful pedestal? When woman has been degraded—in paganism, in polygamy, in dissoluteness—who has lowered her? Finally, if someone asked you to resolve the question, "Which of the two has done the most harm to the other, woman to man or man to woman?" how would you respond?

In place of that question, as sad as it is difficult, I propose an opposite question to you today: "Which of the two wishes henceforth to do the other the most good?"

## MUTUAL HELPERS

Do you see her, meditative before God, seeking how she can henceforth be for us a helper fit for us? Let us, in her interests, meditate on a similar problem at the feet of the same Savior! Moreover, the principles are the same; only the applications differ. Humility and charity—if we abandon these to woman, what will we have left for ourselves? Humility and charity—what else, then, was the man Jesus Christ?

With holy jealousy for one another, let woman's humility and charity support man, and let man's humility and charity support woman, even as we await the time when all the differences that exist down here will be erased for God's elect under a purer sky and on a regenerate earth. There our humility and charity will glorify for all eternity this Savior God who, doubly our Father, created us in a day of love and saved us in a day of grace!

❦

*godly examples*

# Four Monod Women

Hannah Honyman Monod
(1799–1868)

# Four Monod Women

When Adolphe Monod climbed into the pulpit to preach, he was primarily speaking from God's Word, but the applications he drew from his text were inevitably colored by personal experience. Therefore, at the close of his monograph on *Woman*, it is interesting to consider some of the women who were significant in his own life, based on information drawn from letters and other published material.

We can catch a glimpse of his relationship with his wife and then look at his mother, an older sister, and his unmarried daughter, all of whom exhibit the kind of humility and charity that are the subject of this book.

## Hannah Monod, A Wife's Support

In 1829, while serving as a pastor in Lyon, Adolphe married Hannah Honyman, who was from a Scottish family that had moved there following the fall of Napoleon. Adolphe and Hannah had seven children, six of whom survived to adulthood. Apart from brief mentions, Hannah then fades into the background in accounts of Adolphe's life, and there is an absence of correspondence between them in the public record. Yet even these simple facts testify to her role as a quiet, humble helper, supervising the children and the running of the household. What the facts do not reveal is the depth of Adolphe and Hannah's relationship. For that we rely on Adolphe's letter to a dear friend, written in the midst of a family crisis.[1] In July 1852, Hannah and her eldest daughter, Marie (then about twenty-one years old), were out shopping when Hannah suffered a severe stroke. It is not just the content of the letter that shows how precious Adolphe's wife was to him; it is also the letter's telegraphic style, as faith battles fear in his heart.

> *She is better.—Good friend, faithful friend, my wife is (dare I say was?) gravely ill.*

> *A cerebral stroke, Wednesday, around four o'clock, in the street. Brought home unconscious by Marie (poor Marie!). Her speech lost; no movement or feeling in part of her left side. Imminent danger. My brother Gustave [a physician] said to Frédéric [their oldest brother], who later repeated to me, "There is* a possibility *that she will come back from it!"* To see her die and die without communicating with me, oh my friend! My soul melts in anguish!

> *That same evening the most serious symptoms stopped. They disappeared gradually. Gustave took heart beginning Wednesday evening. Thursday midday, a consultation. Mr. Rayer [a specialist] considered the case to be quite serious, almost desperate. Friday, notable improvement, according to Mr. Rayer himself. The best persists.*

> *My children and I were kept* in peace. *We, I too, I had* absolutely no bitterness. *I considered that God was just if he struck and good if he spared. . . .*

---

[1] Sarah Monod, *Adolphe Monod, Souvenirs de Sa Vie, Extraits de Sa Correspondance* (Paris : Librairie Fischbacher, 1885), pp 365–366.

*Pray for us and keep on praying. I still don't dare give myself over to hope. Imagine poor Adolphe Monod without his life's companion, the pillar of his home, the helper of his ministry, the balance in his advice, the dear friend of his heart, and the mother of his children! . . . Farewell. If "we live," I will write to you again in a few days.*

What wife would not inwardly rejoice to hear herself described in such terms! Hannah did recover and lived another sixteen years, twelve years longer than her husband. She never regained her full strength but was able to resume a normal life. She even translated Adolphe's deathbed meditations, *Les Adieux,* and his sermons on *Jesus Tempted in the Wilderness* into English. She truly was "a helper fit for" her husband.

## LOUISE MONOD,
## A MOTHER'S INVOLVEMENT

Adolphe Monod was one of twelve siblings, all of whom lived to be adults. He was the sixth to be born and the first to die. Louise Monod's faith, like that of her pastor husband, was more formal than vibrant, yet she had a strong influence for godliness on her children. She took just the kind of deep and active interest in their lives that Adolphe advocates. As a result, her children felt they could continue to confide in her and seek her counsel, long after they had left the family home. And she could confide in them.

During the years that Adolphe and his brother Billy, two years his senior, were in seminary together in Geneva, they took turns writing in a diary that was sent to their mother. At the beginning of their studies they wrote:

*Here, dear Mama, is the beginning of the journal that you asked us for. . . . Each evening, before we go to bed, we will take turns writing here, in just a few words, the events of the day, down to the smallest details, even down to our most intimate troubles and pleasures, our contentment, our reproaches, our most secret feelings. By "secret," I mean that which we would not even confide to our most intimate friends. Yet where it concerns our parents, our beloved parents, we have nothing to hide, and this journal will be the proof of it. This good mother has promised to read with interest all these little details, and how would it not be a true pleasure for us to converse every day with her this way and to open the secrets of our hearts to her?* [2]

This they did, leaving a detailed record of all that went on during their student days. Then as their studies ended and they were consecrated to the gospel ministry, they immediately thought of their mother, still in Paris. Adolphe wrote:

*Here we are; just a moment ago we became ministers. Before anything else, since we cannot have the pleasure of sharing this day with you, I need to tell you, my angel of a mother, the thoughts and feelings that occupy me. My father is here with us, we are very happy, and the only thing still lacking will be found again in Paris in a few weeks. As for me, I sense that I was wiser on this occasion than I typically am in times of religious solemnity or strong emotion.*

*You know how I spoil these lovely moments through my scruples and anxiety. Even yesterday evening I experienced a feeling of fear and sadness at the thought of the approaching day. Yet the good advice I received, good reflection, a talk with my father—these restored me to a better disposition, thanks be to God. While the sense of my weakness makes me grave and serious, it doesn't make me sad. I hope, I believe, I know that since God has blessed our work and has visibly led us, right up to this entrance into our career, he will not abandon us at the most important moment of our lives.* [3]

---

[2] *Souvenirs*, pp 19–20.
[3] *Souvenirs*, pp 49–50.

Then, as Adolphe went through his years of spiritual crisis while leading a small church in Naples, his mother wrote, *You have been always, each moment, the object of my concern and my most fervent prayers.*[4] Her prayers and those of other family members (as we shall see below) were answered when Adolphe Monod met God personally. Soon, however, their situations were reversed. It was his mother who sensed the need for a deeper, more vibrant faith. Five months after Adolphe's conversion and shortly after his move to Lyon to take on an important pastoral position there, she wrote him a letter opening her heart to him. She was in her husband's office early on a Sunday morning, when she alone in the household was awake.

*I bless God, my Adolphe, for the help he has granted you. May he continue to sustain you, watch over your health, and cause you to find happiness in fulfilling the duties that are placed upon you. You will fulfill these not only with zeal, but with a satisfaction that will fill up at least a part of the emptiness your poor heart is experiencing in these first moments.*

*You were happily inspired in giving the sermon of preparation [for communion] that gave us so much pleasure. I would truly like to hear it from your lips today, as I get ready to take communion with a soul that is, alas, ill prepared to do so. I suffer from sadness and discouragement at the thought of my unworthiness, at the thought of how my time is spent, the way my whole life has been spent. What great need I have of the grace and mercy of my God!*

*I do not despair, but I astonish myself in daring to count on that grace when I think of my coldness, my ingratitude, and my distractions throughout this long life. Life for me has been so filled with blessings of every type and help of every kind, yet it has been so empty of love for*

---

[4] *Souvenirs*, p 93.

*God, of confidence in my Savior, of charity, and of good
works! May I at least not approach the sacred Table
unworthily! It is painful to me never to go with the joy that
should characterize every true Christian. Pray for me, my
cherished son. I count much on the prayers of my children.
More fortunate than I, they will not have waited until the
end of their course to think of giving their hearts to God.*[5]

She did, ultimately, give her heart to God. He answered
her prayers and those of her children. The blessing came full
circle. Though we are not told just how or when the change
happened, it is clear that, at the time of her death twenty four
years later, Louise Monod's faith was lively and strong.
During her last, brief illness, she asked her children and
grandchildren to write out verses of Scripture for her, and
she read over these regularly. Yet on the very day of her
death she remarked, *It seems that nobody has given me, "I have
blotted out your transgressions like a cloud and your sins like mist"*[6]
(Isaiah 44:22), and she asked that this be added to the list.
Her children had this verse engraved on her tombstone. She
also said, *May it please the Lord to shorten things, but whatever he
wishes. I am his. He has redeemed me. I am at peace.*[7]

## ADÈLE MONOD BABUT,
## AN OLDER SISTER'S EXAMPLE

Adolphe Monod points out that young daughters still
living in the parental home can prepare themselves for wom-
anhood by being of practical and, especially, spiritual help to
their younger siblings. Apparently Adèle Monod did just that,

---

[5] *Souvenirs*, pp 133–134.
[6] *Souvenirs*, p 349.
[7] *Souvenirs*, p 350.

and she seems to have had a particularly close relationship with Adolphe, who was five years her junior. Later, after Adèle had married Édouard Babut and was living in London, Adolphe went through a profound spiritual crisis. Her letters to him during this period bear eloquent testimony to the depth of her faith, the closeness of her relationship with her brother, and her insight into his problems. In May 1825, her daughter and only child, Louise, died at the age of seven months. Then in February 1827 a second daughter, just six months old, also died. Here are excerpts from a remarkable letter Adèle wrote just three days later.

*She is no more, my dear Adolphe; at least she is no more for us in this world, this beloved little Marie, source of so many consolations, joys, and hopes. Sometimes it seemed to me that my Louise had been given back to me; now I seem to have lost her a second time. Dear Adolphe, how wrenching is the agony through which I have just passed once again. How painful is the void left by the loss of a being so tenderly loved and who already was giving so much happiness! . . .*

*Adolphe, in this solemn moment, I thought also of you. No doubt it was God who, in his infinite goodness, said to my torn soul that it could also receive blessing on your behalf, that the anguish of your poor sister could be the source of the Christian peace that we ask for you with such fervor. Dear Adolphe, if I am not mistaken, if my daughter in her death could preach to you with more eloquence and conviction than all those who have been seeking your good, ah, how true it would be to say that the day of her death has greater value than the day of her birth. I would thank God for all I have suffered. The thought of the happiness of my daughters and of the happy change in my dear Adolphe would alone remain in my heart and would give me the strength to resign myself to all that may still await me, convinced that no sorrow would be too much to pay for such a great benefit.*

*You will perhaps be astounded at the hope I base on my unhappiness. I don't know, my friend, but something tells me you will feel led to love the religion that consoles and sustains your unfortunate sister, that you will recognize this faith that can calm the anguish of a mother whose dearest hopes have three times been reversed as coming from heaven, and that you will worship this charitable Redeemer who saves me from despair and murmuring [and] who has gathered my children into his bosom. . . .*

*Oh, in these days of misery and mourning, what would I become without him! If he is not alive, if his words are not eternally true, where can we draw strength against so many sorrows? But may he be blessed for the conviction he places in my soul. Oh, may he deign to make it pass into yours as well!*

*Adolphe, dear Adolphe, give him your heart. Love him for the good that he does for me, while waiting to love him for the good he will do for you, once you come to him with humility and simplicity of heart. Do not seek to understand him; you will understand him enough once you have learned to love him. And how could you not be grateful for his mercy toward me, you who have always been so tenderly attached to me!* [8]

Her last advice, "Do not seek to understand him," shows how well Adèle understood her brother. That is just what he was trying to do. Adolphe's reaction to this letter was expressed to his mother. *I received Adèle's letter. I have no words for the admiration she inspires in me. This is the ultimate in charity! How fortunate she is! How fortunate! I will, no doubt, answer her tomorrow or Thursday, but what will I say to her? Oh, my God, courage! I will tell her the truth, such as it is in my heart.* [9]

---

[8] *Souvenirs*, pp 102–105.
[9] *Souvenirs*, p 106.

Eventually he wrote Adèle a lengthy reply, expressing how much he wished he could tell her what she longed to hear. Then in July, after the dramatic encounter with God that ended his spiritual crisis, one of his first letters was to this beloved older sister, sharing at great length his new joy and peace.

*My tender and beloved Adèle, you are a sister who has pushed fraternal love and Christian charity toward me to the point of finding consolation in the death of her only child. If God used the rending of her heart to restore peace to mine, such a sister has first rights to be told immediately of the first steps God has caused me to take in Christian peace. That is why, my tender and beloved sister, having waited only the time necessary to assure myself that what is happening in me is not a working of my natural capriciousness but an operation of the One in whom there is no shadow of turning, I come to give you the best of news about me.*

*You will have known from my letter that during the last five months I had made no progress. . . . In reading the gospel, I forgot that I could neither understand nor receive it unless God himself prepared my spirit. Therefore I was impatient to grasp it all at once. . . . Then, seeing as if by a shaft of light that my spirit was and always had been in a state of blindness and wandering that had to cease if I were to have peace, . . . and seeing that I thus had no hope save in an* external influence, *I remembered the promise of the Holy Spirit. Learning in the end through necessity that of which the positive statements of the gospel had been unable to persuade me,* for the first time in my life *I believed in that promise in the only way it could best speak to the needs of my soul. I believed in it as a real, external, supernatural action . . . exerted over me by a God who is the master of my heart as truly as he is the master of nature. . . . Renouncing all merit, all strength, all personal resource, and recognizing in myself no claim on his mercy other than my misery, I asked him for his Spirit in order to change mine.*[10]

## SARAH MONOD,
## A SINGLE WOMAN'S SERVICE

Sarah was the fourth of Adolphe and Hannah Monod's seven children. Of the six who lived into adulthood, she is the only one who never married. True to her father's teaching, she used her single status to be of immense service to her family and, ultimately, to God's kingdom, by preserving much precious information about her father's life. On behalf of her siblings and for the benefit of her nieces and nephews, she apparently did most of the work in compiling two large volumes from Adolphe Monod's correspondence and diaries. The first volume *Souvenirs de Sa Vie, Extraits de Sa Correspondance* is tied together by her narrative on his life. It was published in 1885, nearly thirty years after his death.

Always in that spirit of humility that Adolphe says is appropriate for woman, Sarah fades into the background. It is "we" (his children) who are preparing this remembrance. Her initials (S.M.) at the end of the preface are all that betray her identity. Yet that preface also reveals her own sincere faith, her deep affection for her father, and her spirit of service to the family.

> *One need not seek a real biography in the pages that follow. Even if we had the desire to give one to the public, a legitimate concern would restrain us. During his last illness, Adolphe Monod himself advised those around him not to write one. Not that he intended to forbid them from doing so, but he felt that his life did not offer enough salient events to furnish the material for a biography. Our goal then has sim-*

---

[10] *Souvenirs*, pp 117–120.

ply been to assemble and organize a few memories of his life, such as are suitable for establishing his image and necessary for understanding his correspondence, while allowing him to speak for himself, as much as possible.

For those who have only known him in the pulpit or through his writings, we hope there will be more than just an interest born of curiosity and affection in seeing him in everyday life. Besides, it is beneficial to consider men such as him in the context of their personal lives. His character only grows as we examine it more closely, or rather as we learn how to discern the unique well from which he drew the strength of his eloquence and the humility and charity that became the distinctive traits of his Christian character.

There are also souls who are burdened, as his was for many years, by a sense of sin and by an immense need for pardon and holiness. Therefore it is useful, particularly perhaps in our day, for them to see how God used all of his moral suffering and internal struggles both to lead him to seek truth in his Word alone—and seek it with the simplicity of a child—and to propel him to the foot of the cross of Jesus Christ, where he remained until the end of his life. . . .

To truly respect his memory and enter into the spirit that animated him, we in no way seek to exalt the glory of the man. Rather, through the simple recounting of what God did in him, for him, and through him, we desire to bear witness to God's faithfulness and give glory to his goodness. . . .

Our intention is not to elaborate on [Adolphe Monod's] writings or preaching, any more than it is to judge or weigh his conduct and ecclesiastical principles—things that would comprise the body of an ordinary biography. What is to be said on these subjects will be heard from him. Here we are in full agreement with M. le professeur Pédézert, who wrote, "He deserves to be considered apart and for himself, but only one man can speak fittingly of him, and he is that man."

A perfect honesty obliges us not to exclude from our collection such letters as might seem, if not contradictory, at least as indicating certain changes in the views or thinking of their author. Are not these changes themselves part of his moral history, and was he not the first to recognize that his ideas, or the form in which he believed he should clothe them, might have changed on this or that point, even though these changes have sometimes been exaggerated?

On the other hand, we will be pardoned for not fearing, from time to time, to mention certain intimate or familiar details. If an excuse were needed, we would find it in the very dedication to this volume, "to Adolphe Monod's grandchildren," none of whom had the privilege of knowing their grandfather. We will be happy if, effacing ourselves in order to bring this austere, tender, and holy figure back to life for them, we can communicate to them some spark of his love for the truth and of his zeal for the salvation of souls and for the glory of God!

Let us again record those words written by him at the beginning of one of his discourses, words that are like the key to his ministry and life. "Oh my Savior God, assist me, for your glory and for the honor of your holy Son Jesus! My heart, my spirit, my soul, my body, my voice, my pen—I place all under your keeping and at your exclusive disposition!"

S. M. [11]

---

[11] *Souvenirs*, pp VII–XIII.

## MONOD GENEALOGY

Jean Monod (1765–1836) = **Louise de Coninck** (1775–1851)

  Frédéric Monod (1794–1863) = Constance de Coninck
                              = Suzanne Smedley
  Henri Monod (1795–1869) = Camille Gros
  **Adèle Monod** (1796–1876) = Edouard Babut
  Edouard Monod (1798–1887) = Elisa Gros
  Guillaume Monod (1800–1896) = Sophie Peschier-Vieusseux
                              = Nina Lauront
  **Adolphe Monod** (1802–1856) = **Hannah Honyman**

    Marie Monod (1831–1890) = Henri Morin
    Marguerite Monod (1832–1887) = Auguste Bouvier
    André John William Monod (1834–1916) = Marie Valette
    **Sarah Monod** (1838–1912)
    Emilie Monod (1838–1920) = Théodore Audeoud
    Constance Monod (1840–1841)
    Camille Monod (1843–1910) = Charles Félix Vernes

  Gustave Monod (1803–1890) = Jane Good
  Valdemar Monod (1807–1870) = Adèle le Cavelier
  Marie Suzanne Monod (1809–1886) = Charles-Louis Stapfer
  Horace Monod (1814–1881) = Suzanne Gardes
  Elisa Monod (1815–1867)
  Marie Cécile Monod (1818–?)

# OTHER TITLES FROM SOLID GROUND

In addition to Monod's *Woman* and the other Monod Classics listed at the front of this edition, Solid Ground Christian Books has reprinted several volumes from the Puritan era, such as:

*The Complete Works of Thomas Manton* (in 22 volumes)
*A Body of Divinity* by Archbishop James Ussher
*An Exposition of Hebrews* by William Gouge
*A Short Explanation of Hebrews* by David Dickson
*An Exposition of the Epistle of Jude* by Thomas Jenkyn
*A Commentary on the New Testament* by John Trapp
*Gospel Sonnets* by Ralph Erskine
*Heaven Upon Earth* by James Janeway
*The Marrow of True Justification* by Benjamin Keach
*The Travels of True Godliness* by Benjamin Keach
*The Redeemer's Tears Wept Over Lost Souls* by John Howe
*Commentary on the Second Epistle of Peter* by Thomas Adams
*The Christian Warfare* by John Downame
*An Exposition of the Ten Commandments* by Ezekiel Hopkins
*The Harmony of the Divine Attributes* by William Bates
*The Communicant's Companion* by Matthew Henry
*The Secret of Communion with God* by Matthew Henry

View at www.solid-ground-books.com

Call us at 205-443-0311